Reindeer Reflections

REINDEER REFLECTIONS

Lessons from an Ancient Culture

JERRY HAIGH

FOREWORD BY YANN MARTEL

RMB

For information on purchasing bulk quantities of this book, or to obtain media excerpts or invite the author to speak at an event, please visit rmbooks.com and select the "Contact" tab.

RMB | Rocky Mountain Books Ltd.
rmbooks.com
@rmbooks
facebook.com/rmbooks

Cataloguing data available from Library and Archives Canada
ISBN 9781771605151 (hardcover)
ISBN 9781771605168 (electronic)

All photographs are by Jerry Haigh unless otherwise noted.
Maps by Tayyab Ikram Shah, University of Saskatchewan.

Printed and bound in Canada

We would like to also take this opportunity to acknowledge the traditional territories upon which we live and work. In Calgary, Alberta, we acknowledge the Niitsítapi (Blackfoot) and the people of the Treaty 7 region in Southern Alberta, which includes the Siksika, the Piikuni, the Kainai, the Tsuut'ina, and the Stoney Nakoda First Nations, including Chiniki, Bearpaw, and Wesley First Nations. The City of Calgary is also home to Métis Nation of Alberta, Region III. In Victoria, British Columbia, we acknowledge the traditional territories of the Lkwungen (Esquimalt and Songhees), Malahat, Pacheedaht, Scia'new, T'Sou-ke, and W̱SÁNEĆ (Pauquachin, Tsartlip, Tsawout, Tseycum) peoples.

We acknowledge the financial support of the Government of Canada through the Canada Book Fund and the Canada Council for the Arts, and of the province of British Columbia through the British Columbia Arts Council and the Book Publishing Tax Credit.

FOR JO, AS EVER

The best thing to hold onto in life is each other.
—AUDREY HEPBURN

The cure for boredom is curiosity.
There is no cure for curiosity.
—DOROTHY PARKER

I live in Saskatoon, the prairie city in Treaty 6 Territory.
A place where people have gathered to listen and share stories
since time immemorial. It is the home of the Cree, Dene,
Anishinaabe, Dakota, Lakota and Nakota People
and the homeland of the Metis.

CONTENTS

Part Three — Results and Conclusions of the Work in Mongolia

Foreword

On the basis of a single book of mine, some people think I'm an "animal guy." It's true that I did my share of research. I read books, watched movies, travelled, talked to people and took lots of notes. I did everything I needed to get the story right. But that's it. My ignorance of the animal world, a plunging abyss, starts just beyond the edge of every paragraph in *Life of Pi*.

Jerry Haigh is something else. He truly is an animal guy. A wildlife vet at the University of Saskatchewan for over 30 years, and before that working ten years in Africa with wildlife. To write his books, he has combined extensive research with the delight of kicking back and just *remembering*.

He has spent his whole adult life on that porous border where animals and humans meet. His interest in the many other species with which we share this planet has been abiding and constant, the inspiration for all his work.

Reindeer Reflections is the latest expression of this interest. In this book, there is much about reindeer, or caribou as we call them in North America. (Did you know that, reader, that caribou and reindeer are the same thing? Did you really? I bet you didn't.) Reindeer in Scandinavia, reindeer in Mongolia, reindeer in Russia and Alaska and Saskatchewan, reindeer everywhere, with even a little detour to talk about Santa's reindeer. But the book goes deeper than that, because, of course, when we talk about animals, we're never *only* talking about animals. We're also talking about ourselves. We *see* ourselves through animals; we see our commonalities and our distinction. We see that we have never entirely left Noah's Ark but still live with them in a mysterious communion that continues to fascinate. In looking at animals, we see the best of ourselves, and the worst — a capacity to live in harmony, and to destroy.

So this is not just a book about animals, but about people, specifically, most memorably, the reindeer herders of Mongolia. You will learn about reindeer and about the Tsaatan People. But you will also learn about yourself.

Jerry is a genial, relaxed storyteller. His stories, anchored in zoological facts, are peppered with humour and insights. I invite you to share the pleasure I had in reading about his adventures.

—Yann Martel

Preface

There are many accounts of the domestication of wild animals by humans. Reindeer are of that history. Reindeer and caribou are one and the same species, so called depending on where they live. Wild reindeer in Eurasia, wild caribou in North America. Domestic ones everywhere. They have the same taxonomic name: *Rangifer tarandus.* Just like makes of vehicles, or minor variations in recipes, there are further distinctions based on size, the regions in which they live and other factors such as their DNA profiles.[1]

The chapters in this book start with the move from Kenya, where I was born and worked for ten years, to Canada. It was in Africa that my career shifted from being a general practitioner to a wildlife vet.

The stories continue to tell of the history, culture and association of domestic reindeer in each society, from the millennia-deep connection with the animals in Mongolia to the

---

1   For easier reading, I have only used "caribou" when mentioning the North American members of the species or referring to the work of others who use it. Mentions of "reindeer" cover both names. Whenever domestic ones are referred to I make it clear.

decades-long relationship in North America.

It was in Saskatoon, as a member of the faculty at Western College of Veterinary Medicine, that I started work on caribou at the local zoo. Not long after my arrival came involvement in research programs with them and many other species of wildlife across the country. African experiences helped with caribou work in an unexpected way.

There are descriptions of visits to Finland and Mongolia where I worked with domestic reindeer. Later chapters cover the results of our studies of artificial insemination and disease issues in reindeer herds. Finally, there are accounts of the rapid declines in numbers of wild and domestic populations, the issues of predation and poaching, and the effects of the COVID-19 pandemic.

Some Notes on Spelling

The Mongolian language is written in Cyrillic. For instance, Монгол becomes Mongolia. Further translation into English can create confusion. A couple of examples among many translated versions are the names of the capital, and of the country's largest lake that lies in the northwest, a few kilometres east of the mountain home of the nomadic reindeer herders where I worked.

The capital city, in Cyrillic, is Улаанбаатар. In English, it is Ulaanbaatar, usually abbreviated as UB. It can also be found as Ulaan Baatar, or even the original Latin script name of the city, Ulan Bator.

The largest lake in Mongolia, Хөвсгөл нуур, or Höwsgöl núr, is variously rendered as Huvsgul, Hovsgol, Hövsgöl or Khövsgöl. I have used Hovsgol.

The village of Tsagaan Nuur, which is named several times in the book, appears in recent maps as Gurvansaikhan.

Most folks I met in the early 2000s used only a single name, a practice I stuck with in the book as well. Dr. Nansalmaa, a veterinarian, and Byamba our translator are examples. Nowadays these two people use their full names, Nansalmaa Myagmar and Byambadorj Altankhuyag, respectively.

The nomadic reindeer herders are either known as the Tsaatan or Dukha. The former translates as "Reindeer People." The Tsaatan is what I use except when quoting others who have used the name Dukha. An older and more accurate name, no longer in use but preferred by members of the culture, is Tsaachin, which literally means "reindeer herder."

Part One

KENYA TO CANADA:

RHINOS TO REINDEER

CHAPTER 1

New Beginnings

My first day in Saskatoon in 1975 passed in the stupor of jetlag after the long flights from Kenya to Europe and then across the Atlantic. All I wanted to do was pay a visit to the vet college, meet Dr. Ole Nielsen, the dean, and my new head of department, Dr. Bill Adams. Nothing more. After a chat to introduce ourselves, Dr. Adams took me to the department coffee lounge where I met some new colleagues. We then did a tour of the place: the buffeteria, the various department offices, the necropsy area, the small and large animal clinics and the library. After a short while, feeling exhausted, I excused myself and headed back to the hotel for an hour or so of catch-up sleep. I knew I needed to go back and find out more about the work, but the hour or so turned into six.

Five in the afternoon meant there would be nobody working at the vet college, and therefore no point in going back. One look out the hotel window persuaded me that a walk along the riverbank might give me a boost and some relaxation from the stresses of the last while, not just the uprooting from my home and friends of ten years but the challenges ahead. They would include figuring out the internal politics at the college, the work on new species and finding a home.

The leaves of the trees were starting to turn to beautiful russets and gold of autumn. Some had already fallen, so, as I absentmindedly scuffed along, listening to the rustle, I mused on those changes ahead. The gentle gurgling water of the South Saskatchewan added a soothing background. The traffic sounds were a distant blur until a teenager roared past in a souped-up car. It had colourful swirls and circles painted on the sides and rear tires half as big again as the front ones.

Next morning, at 4:00 a.m., the jetlag still at work, I read and dozed until breakfast. An obvious priority was a visit to the zoo to meet the staff. I needed to know what I was going to be dealing with. Fully awake after tea and pancakes smeared with butter topped with maple syrup (a first experience), I headed over the river bridge and walked to the college. A monster mustard-yellow Chevy Impala, sitting in the parking lot, had been provided for my exclusive use. A call to the zoo followed by a visit was quickly organized. Making sure that I drove on the right side of the road (also a first), I headed the four kilometres to the park. Brent Pendleton, the zoo foreman, to whom I had spoken, was ready and waiting at the office. His red hair and beard were the first things I noted. We introduced ourselves and headed out to the grounds.

In the animal area we walked past two pens holding different species. They were about 40 by 25 metres, surrounded by a just-over-two-metre page wire fence. Five fallow deer in the first. In the second, half a dozen big gray sheep, the male's horns spiralling out like the bottom of a bedspring from the thick base on his skull in a majestic curve that ended in a point well past the 360-degree turn.

Brent said, "These are Rocky Mountain bighorn sheep. Don't know if you've ever seen them, but like some other kinds they have hair, not wool."

Then a puzzle. Standing in the middle of a pen were two female reindeer. But the black letters on the small, silver-coloured panel told me they were caribou. I'd never even heard of them. Was this a mistake? Surely not. They were reindeer. No doubt about it. Like millions of children worldwide, I knew what reindeer looked like. The pale, gray-coloured coats and small antlers exactly fitted those early images of Christmas scenes. Rudolph, Blitzen, Donner and the rest of Santa's flying team.

Brent explained, "They're the same. It just depends where they're from. All across Europe and Russia, they're reindeer. Here — caribou. Same species, different name."

Another look at the description, particularly the map, showed that caribou exist right across North America, from Alaska to the Eastern Arctic. The most southerly part of the range appeared as a not quite straight line that wandered across Canada as if drawn by an inebriated ant. The line passed through the northern part of my new home province. Interesting.

We walked on. Elk, bison, mule deer, white-tailed deer and others were just as intriguing.

There were two things that needed attention. First and foremost: foot trims. Second, vaccinations of just about everything in the collection. Worst of all, the hoof overgrowth cases were in the mouflon sheep, natives of the Mediterranean island of Corsica. The ram's hooves were some 15 centimetres long, about three times normal. The caribou's were almost as bad.

There was one problem. These caribou were from wild stock. They were not going to stand and allow me to pick up each leg as if they were horses. There was no way to get hold of them. Their shelter stood in the middle of the pen. Whoever had designed the layout of all the enclosures had almost certainly come from a town planning background. A house in the middle of a garden. A fence around the perimeter. All well and good for humans, useless as tits on a boar when it came to rounding up animals that didn't want to be rounded up. They could simply run circles round the shed, leaving frustrated humans looking stupid.

It meant that the caribou would have to be sedated. Not just sedated. They would have to go down and be anaesthetized enough so that we could work without risking an injury from a flying hoof. We needed about ten minutes. It was just as vital to be sure that the patients would fully recover. Anything but a residual mild sedation would be bad news. They might injure themselves in some way, or return to the immobilized state and even stop breathing.

It came down to drugs. What drugs? With ten years of experience in Africa, I had developed a cocktail that worked well. Its main ingredient was the narcotic fentanyl.[2] Mixed with a small dose of a sedative, I had immobilized many dozens of creatures including rhino, elephants and various hoofed animals. A specific antagonist reversed the effects within a minute. Would that cocktail work here? I found out the name of a colleague at the Calgary Zoo and called him for advice and comment. He told me that something similar did the job for him.

It wasn't just a question of the drugs. They had to be administered. It was not Fido, the pet dog, sitting on the exam room table getting his annual shots.

There had to be a way of getting close to the caribou so I could fire a dart into the heavy muscles of the hind end with a less than accurate gun. A shot into the chest or directly onto a bone might not be safe. It might even cause serious damage. A broken bone would be a disaster for the patient. Also a terrible way to start my new career.

The approach was easily solved. I hitched a ride with Jureen,

---

2   What a terrible development in today's world it is that fentanyl has become such a deadly scourge on the streets, killing thousands of addicts when mixed with less potent opioids by unscrupulous dealers.

the grizzled, coverall-clad keeper driving the blue Ford tractor pulling a trailer loaded with hay and oats. He went into all the hoofstock enclosures on a regular basis. Rather than moving away, the caribou came up, looking for their daily goodies. From the trailer, using a gas-powered pistol, I could hardly miss at two metres.

My first trial with the cocktail was 80 per cent successful. The animals did go down and the trimming was easily accomplished. The other 20 per cent was an odd side effect, something I had never seen before but had read about. In the short time between the dart injection and the gentle subsidence to the ground, they both tried to taste-test the rubber steering wheel. Sort of spaced out. Rubber is an unusual meal for anyone.

The "Sunday" name for this behaviour is *allotriophagia* — an uncontrollable impulse to eat unnatural objects. Certainly weird, potentially dangerous if the object happens to be something sharp or toxic.

The hooves were easily dealt with. A few snips with clippers designed for horses, but just as effective here, a rasp to smooth off the edges, and all four feet back to normal.

After that peculiar trial result, I switched to a different additive in the cocktail. A tiny amount of well-known cattle sedative combined with the fentanyl did the perfect job. This combination served well on many other North American species in the following years. Hoofed stock from moose to sheep and deer, plus three species of bear (black, grizzly and polar).

I headed back to the college, musing about the reindeer/caribou question. Did it really matter? Surely, it was not that simple. Caribou here, reindeer in Eurasia. What more was there to learn?

The obvious solution was to go upstairs to the library and find the right book. I was soon learning about them from Banfield's *The Mammals of Canada*. In six informative pages the terms are used interchangeably. The heading reads, "REINDEER or CARIBOU."

Reindeer and caribou have the same taxonomic name — *Rangifer tarandus*. There are subtypes (subspecies) after this pair of names, just like all Honda Accord cars are all Honda Accords but have their own model names. (The 2018 "subspecies" of this car came with 17 different designations, 2.4 litre, Sport, Touring and so on.) There are different mentions of *Rangifer tarandus* subspecies. They range from 14 to 19, woodland, barren ground, Peary and others. With refinements in DNA technology, this number could change, up or down.

In Eurasia all are reindeer. The wild ones are just as wild as the caribou of North America. The difference is that across Eurasia there are also domesticated reindeer. There are some reindeer in North America that are descendants of ones that arrived from Russia in the late 1800s.

They were brought in after a ship's captain, Michael Healy, who traded extensively along both the Russian and Alaskan shores of the Bering Sea, reported that Alaskan Indigenous People were starving. This had happened due to excessive harvesting of marine mammals like seals and walruses by commercial whalers and their ilk.

Captain Healy had witnessed the successful management of domestic reindeer in Russia and reported the dire situation to the commissioner of education in Alaska, Dr. Sheldon Jackson. Healy suggested the idea of transporting some from Siberia to western Alaska as a solution to food shortages among Indigenous Alaskans.

Captain Healy brought the first group, only 16 animals, in 1891. They were unloaded at Amaknak Island to see if they would survive the voyage and the winter. They did. In 1892 he made five further trips to Siberia and brought a total of 171 reindeer. The descendants of those 171 rapidly rose to over 30,000 head by 1927.

Ten years later it was 640,000.

The brutal winter of 1938–39 caused the death of an untold number of animals. Then came the Second World War. Many young men enlisted and the herding system fell into sharp decline. Dr. Greg Finstad, program manager for the Reindeer Research Program at the University of Alaska, Fairbanks, told me that the estimated number of reindeer in the 1950s was based on wild guesses. The number 50,000 was suggested, but, as he said, it could have been almost any number you can think of. In 2018 Dr. Finstad estimated there were some 15,000 to 20,000 domestic reindeer.

The first successful translocation of reindeer to Canada, starting in 1929, involved an epic six-year trek led by a small band of herders from Alaska to the Mackenzie River delta. Like the Alaskans, the Inuit of the region faced starvation. Some 2,370 of the 3,400 that started the journey arrived at Tuktoyaktuk, on the shores of the Arctic Ocean, 200 kilometres from the border with Alaska, in 1935. Of these, only 10 per cent were from the herd that had originally left. The others were born on the trail.

In the early 20th century, a group of the animals was sent to provide meat for the whalers on the island of South Georgia, deep in the southern Atlantic Ocean, no more than a thousand kilometres from the nearest point in Antarctica. They thrived and the herd grew steadily. In February 2011, a decision was made to eradicate them because of the environmental damage they were causing. In late 2017, the last two of some 6,800 head were shot.

CHAPTER 2

Reindeer Domestication

I have long been fascinated by the subject of animal domestication. How and when did it occur? Which animal was the first?

There are several lists of creatures with astonishing variations in numbers of animals considered to qualify as domestic
animals, all the way from one of only 14 (that does not include
reindeer) to another of nearly 400 that includes Siamese fighting
fish and laboratory mice.

Dr. Finstad of the Reindeer Research Program in Alaska defines
domestication as "the process of genetically manipulating an animal
or plant through artificial selection to better suit the needs of
human beings." He explains, "Animals are considered to be domesticated when they are kept for a distinct purpose, humans control
their breeding, their survival depends on humans, and they develop
traits that are not found in the wild. It's more than simply taming."

When it comes to reindeer, the genetic components include
changes such as the shortened broad head, prominent forehead,
shortened limbs and calmness. There are also changes in coat
colours. They include piebald and spotted reindeer, and the

millennial long-term selection of white-coloured animals chosen as totem animals by the Tsaatan herders of Mongolia.

In the broader picture, humans have meddled with other, now-domesticated animals. There is a general consensus that dogs, used for hunting, were the first domesticated creatures, about 15,000 years ago. Then came goats, pigs and sheep some 12,000 years ago. Humans domesticated chickens, likely bred from the jungle cock of Asia, at about the same time.

When people domesticated wild animals, an astonishing variety of tame versions slowly resulted. The dog is the best-known example. From wolf to Irish wolfhound to the pocket poodle, dogs exemplify the power humans have when they take control of the breeding of a species.

A remarkable example of the transition an animal goes through during domestication is that of the foxes that went from truly wild to domestic in seven generations. In 1959 Soviet scientist Dmitry Belyayev began an experiment in which he selected wild-caught foxes for breeding based solely on their behaviour towards humans. He categorized them according to their degree of tameness. He then bred tame to tame and selected again. The seventh generation of pups wagged their tails and bonded with people within a few days of birth.

A recent example has been demonstrated by leading deer scientist and author Dr. John Fletcher.

In New Zealand red deer and the closely related wapiti were captured from the wild and fenced. Farmed North American elk (wapiti) were imported in 1980 and used in crossbreeding programs with the red deer. The deer can be handled with ease, and artificial insemination and embryo transfer are standard procedures on many farms. In little over 40 years, red deer and their wapiti crosses have become an important part of the agricultural economy of New Zealand. They are also farmed in North America and Europe.

Domestication of reindeer certainly started a long time ago, but we may never know the exact era during which the transition from wild to domestic occurred. There is credible information that it may have started at the same time as it did with dogs. Another opinion comes from Professor Piers Vitebsky of Cambridge University, who lived and worked with the Eveny People of Siberia. He wrote, in his fascinating 2005 book, *The Reindeer People*, that the practice may be at least 3,000 years old: "Nobody knows when or how this [domestication] was done." Studies from the 1940s suggest that reindeer domestication by the people who live in the Sayan Mountains of what is now southern Russia and north-western Mongolia may have occurred at least 5,000 years ago, and that they were likely the first people to do it. There are also suggestions that it may be as little as 2,000 years ago. These widely separated dates almost certainly reflect that, from the start, early hunters followed the wild herds and found ways to influence their behaviour. The caribou of North America have never been domesticated.

The question of "when" can only be estimated. The intriguing thing is the "how." How did those wild reindeer of Eurasia become domesticated? It could have involved a variety of methods. The use of decoy animals to attract and trap is the most likely method, but how were those first decoys captured and domesticated?

The process would almost certainly have been associated with hunting and the need for sustenance. Wild reindeer were a major source of food, clothing, shelter and other material such as sinews for stitching. The winter coat is one of the very best natural materials for insulation, vital during harsh weather when temperatures can plummet and stay in the minus temperature range, as low as minus 50°C, for long periods. In winter the meat would freeze and be available for long periods.

The hunters would have noticed that some members of a herd were flighty and others stayed with the main group. They would have chosen to start domestication with those that did not flee, and in that way gradually acclimatize them to become domestic and then line breed them through generations, just as is done with cattle, horses and others livestock.

Among those were animals that would approach a bait of offered salt. It's a vital part of animal diet and is routinely offered to livestock everywhere. Without it, survival would be impossible. It has been traded all over the world for thousands of years. In conversation with explorer Wilfred Thesiger, I learned it was removed in slabs from the Danakil Depression in Ethiopia and transported to market on the backs of camels. At one time it was the coin of the realm there. I have sat and watched it being extracted by owners of small pans in Uganda's Lake Katwe. The pans, each one owned by a family, are divided by mud walls. Under the equatorial sun, the water, four times as salty as the average of the world's oceans, evaporates and the salt precipitates to the bottom of the pan. It is then shovelled out and piled on the walls, loaded onto donkey carts and taken to market. It's an important source of income for the villagers.

In the reindeer case, it's not salt that is extracted from lakes or mines but salt in urine. In far northern winters, snow is the only source of water for both the humans and animals, and they need a regular supply of water. At that time, reindeer feed almost exclusively on lichens because the other plants they use in summer are no longer available. The quantity of salt in lichens varies a bit according to the species, but is minute in all. The animals have been observed eating snow where others have urinated. Urine contains a wide range of chemicals, many essential to survival. Salt is one of them. Those hunters, consummate naturalists, would have observed the craving for it and used their own to bring the deer ever closer, gradually, perhaps over months, developing a bond to the point at which the reindeer not only waited for their salt source but recognized that people offered defence against predators.

Professor Vitebsky wrote that the Evenki (closely related to the Eveny), one of the largest herding groups in Siberia, have a legend telling how

> a woman noticed that female reindeer and their calves would eat the moss where she had urinated, attracted by the saltiness. The woman continued to urinate nearer to her tent and the reindeer approached closer each time. At length they allowed her to reach out and touch them. When she milked them, she discovered that the milk was delicious.

It may be a legend, but the method is still used. In her wonderful book *The Real Rudolph: A Natural History of Reindeer*, Tilly Smith, co-owner with her husband of the Cairngorm Reindeer Herd in Scotland, recounts how herdsmen of the Chukchi and Koryak Reindeer People would carry a flask of human urine on their belts to attract their deer so as to harness them.

There are other possibilities for the methods that were used to capture and tame the reindeer. Pit traps are one. They are found in many parts of Scandinavia and would have been an efficient method. Smith tells of a series of 500 pits over a distance of only five miles (eight kilometres). Migrating herds could simply enter narrow channels by the use of funnel-shaped wing fences or be forced by humans into them. The wings ended up as narrow channels where the traps were disguised by covers of light vegetation or snow. The animals would fall into the pits and, if the herd were large, those running at the back would press the ones in front that had no chance to escape. A similar method, using corrals at the end of the funnels, might have been used.

The animals could then be killed with spears or arrows. It would be reasonable to think that any calves that survived a fall or corralling could have been recovered alive and domesticated.

Another way to lure wild animals into close human contact is the use of sound. It is still practised. Hunters imitate animal calls to attract potential prey within range. Not just mammals. Waterfowl are easily lured with appropriate whistles, quacks or gaggles, often created with manufactured equipment, even recorded sounds transmitted through speakers. Several reindeer herding peoples can imitate reindeer using a birch bark "trumpet," which lures unsuspecting animals into purpose-built enclosures.

Once those first few deer have been tamed and accepted by the humans, the best method for capturing more remains the use of decoys. They were still used by some herders in Siberia and far-eastern Russia up to at least the 1990s, when Dr. Finstad carried out his detailed studies.

My friend the late Tony Bubenik, consummate biological scientist, working in Alaska in the late 20th century, was able, during the rut, to lure a caribou bull away from a group of females by making a dummy that consisted of an antlered head slung on his shoulders. It would be no surprise to learn that his luring method, a form of decoying, was used thousands of years ago. There is the likelihood of danger when confronted by a rutting bull, so a solution to this element would have to be planned ahead. Dr. Bubenik did it by dropping the dummy, no doubt to the surprise of the bull.

Ha-has are another possible method and could have been used to capture the animals if a decoy had been tethered on the inside. (A ha-ha is a ditch with one vertical wall that is 2.5 metres high, or higher. From the bottom of that wall the other side of the ditch slopes gradually up at a gentle angle over perhaps as much as five or six metres to the level ground.) Animals can jump into the enclosure but cannot leap out from the bottom of the ditch.

Use of one-way gates in fences through which animals can be lured by a tame decoy, or, in the New Zealand example, farmed deer already inside the fence, is another. This simple technique was used in the early days of the deer farming industry there.

An intriguing example is the story of Ohthere, known from a tenth-century manuscript held at the British Library. Ohthere visited the court of King Alfred the Great of Wessex (871–899) in the late ninth century and told the king about his travels in many parts of what is now known as Scandinavia. One of the scholars who recorded the event was Orosius, who described Ohthere's economic resources, including a herd of 600 "tame deer" called *hranas*, or reindeer. Among these were six prized "decoy deer" used to lure wild reindeer into captivity.

Ancient reindeer domestication likely involved most or all of the above techniques, although the process was no doubt much slower than that of Belyayev's fox subjects.

The domestication process can lead to a wide variety of breeds. For instance, using cattle as an example, all are descended from the aurochs, about 8,000 years ago. Texas Longhorn cattle are definitely domestic animals but not exactly tame. The 1600-kilometre (give or take) drives of them, over many days to points north, are at one end of the scale, not wild but not creatures one could walk up to and stroke. Tame, beautiful doe-eyed Jersey cows that have stood with half-closed eyes, obviously enjoying the attention as I scratched them behind the ears, are at the other end.

Domestic reindeer are on a similar gradient.

There are several breeds of reindeer across the northern hemisphere. In western Eurasia, the Sámi and Lapps have developed a breed that is used for sledges, as pack animals and as a milk source. The herding methods also vary. The Sámi of Fenno-Scandinavia and their immediate neighbours on the Russian side of the border, the Samodi, are the only people that use dogs for this purpose. Across northern Russia and Siberia, some reindeer are only used for riding and sledge purposes, others for just riding. Not all milk their animals. In far-eastern Russia, the Chukotka breed are an all-purpose type that can be milked, used as pack animals and harnessed, and are known for meat production and high muscle to bone ratio. It's no surprise to learn that the Alaskan reindeer shipped from that region by Captain Healy 140 years ago, and then some of them trekked to Canada, have similar characteristics.

The Tsaatan of Mongolia have gone two steps further. Their animals are tame from the get-go. They not only enjoy close attention but are milked while free-standing, ridden, harnessed and used as pack animals. I have collected blood from dozens of them while they stood quietly, held with a halter by one person while others stood chatting. Herding is simple and occurs daily. It was no surprise to see people rounding up a group while they rode bareback (on reindeer) with the mob. Once they reached camp, the animals were tethered by short lengths of rope or strips of hide to individual stakes or deadfall trees for the night. They lay down or stood quietly, not struggling. Calves were tied a distance from their mothers to prevent them sucking. This meant there would be milk for the herder to obtain in morning. The cow was then released and, accompanied by her youngster, wandered off to graze.

An example of such docility is the delightful cover of a 1673 publication by Joannis Schefferus about reindeer in Scandinavia that shows a haltered reindeer being led by a couple. It carries a baby in a papoose in a sling on its left-hand side.

Tame reindeer led by halters or harnessed are often seen in Christmas parades. Christmas tree farmers often use them to attract customers. In my pre-retirement days (many moons ago), a client near Saskatoon would go for regular bike rides on the family farm accompanied by her dog on one side and a reindeer on the other, neither of them on any kind of leash.

The most memorable of my experiences with reindeer occurred during my first visit to Mongolia. A young boy, perhaps

10 or 12 years old, threw a blanket over the back of a bull that was grazing about 50 metres from us as we rode by on our horses. He then lifted his right leg up and rolled onto its back and prodded it forwards. In the next camp four reindeer came right up to me, looked and sniffed. It was as if they were thinking, "Who is this guy? Let's check him out."

Another example of gentleness takes full advantage of modern trends. Alaskan Running Reindeer Ranch owner Jane Atkinson wondered if the animals would be a good fit for a yoga class. She took the next logical step. Under the tutelage of employee and qualified yoga instructor Elsa Janney, she gave it a go and set up classes. In a transcript of a National Public Radio transmission, titled "Move Over, Goat Yoga. Alaskans Now Have Reindeer Yoga," reporter Ravenna Koenig quoted participant Tarah Hoxsie: "This is like the ultimate, OK. So while everybody's doing goat yoga in the lower 48, we're doing reindeer yoga, which is way cooler."

Despite the well-known activity of hordes of blood-sucking mosquitos that proliferate in the north in summer and the attacks and drill-like bites of huge *Tabanid* horseflies, known in Canada's north as "bulldogs," two dozen people gathered at a time to exercise on their mats. Meanwhile, the reindeer, used to their role as petting zoo members, were oblivious and stood around, one scratching its ear, another lying down among the yogis.

Unlike other peoples, the Sámi use the term *semi-domesticated* to categorize their animals. In Finland they are considered semi-domesticated. Anne Ollila, executive director of the Finnish Reindeer Herders' Association, put it this way:

> In Finland, reindeer are defined semi-domesticated. Our reindeer calves are born in wild and their first, very short, encounter with people happens usually in summer ear markings, during June — July. Then they meet people again in Autumn round-ups in October

— December. We choose the male calves to training when they are about 9 months old. Then it takes from three to five winters to train them to sleigh work. It takes that long because we let them live free in the nature over summer months. If we would keep them inside corrals year around, the process will surely be a lot shorter. But we see it an animal welfare issue, and choose the longer route. So our "real reindeer" are always free, and also our sleigh working tamed reindeer spend 7–8 months roaming free in the nature and then 4–5 months in a corral, working 3–5 days a week, 2–3 hours per working day.

However, it may not be that simple. Professor Vitebsky also wrote that today it seems impossible to domesticate wild reindeer. He added that if the captured calf of a wild reindeer is tethered, it might struggle and strangle itself or die of exhaustion because it is so desperate to escape. In such cases it may be a matter of the restraint method and an urge to achieve quick results. The decoying, corralling and regular feeding and contact that must have been required in the earliest days was obviously not used by his informants. A rope around the neck of a wild mustang tied to a post would certainly also lead to a violent struggle. Domestication does not occur overnight. The next step, taming, will take daily contact, over many weeks.

If foxes can be turned from wild creatures to pets in seven generations, it comes as no surprise that reindeer behaviour and morphology can be altered from wild to domestic over thousands of years.

Domestic reindeer are livestock. Livestock with antlers, not horns.

While the initial speculations lead to known facts, there are ancient accounts from folklore.

CHAPTER 3

Traditional Tales

While the timing and techniques for reindeer to become domestic animals are not precisely known, there are folk tale explanations for how the relationship between the people and the deer developed.

The first ones I learned are part of the Mongolian Tsaatan folklore tradition. The Tsaatan are nomadic reindeer herders who live in the northwest taiga region.

These herders have origin stories that indicate domestication dating back thousands of years. Morgan Keay, a tall, red-headed American who has been closely associated with them, quotes one that she gleaned in 2002 from a charming herder named Erdenchimeg whom I also met in 2004 and on two subsequent trips into the mountains.

> A poor woman in ancient times was wandering in the mountains without any animals. She came upon a deer and was careful not to disturb it. For three days she returned to the same spot and found the deer

waiting curiously for her. On the third day, there were two deer, and she called to them, "Goo goo goo," and said "If you come home with me, we can take care of each other. I will protect you from wolves and give you salt to eat, and you can give my people food and a way to travel." The deer followed the woman home, and as it was fall, the deer mated, and the first reindeer was soon born.

Another origin story I learnt from Morgan about the Tsaatan has, like so many similar stories for many of the world's cultures, a water component.

A long time ago a huge flood began to rise on the earth. As time went by the waters rose and much of the land was covered. People and reindeer moved ever higher up the mountains until there was nothing else left. The forests were covered as far as the eye could see. The reindeer and the people decided to cooperate in order to survive and soon developed a close relationship. As the water retreated the friendship stayed close and the people moved out into the rest of the world to teach others how to domesticate other animals.

Professor Vitebsky made several trips visiting and living among the Eveny People of Siberia. In *Reindeer People* he shares legends of the origin of domestic reindeer told by the herders and the closely related Evenki People.

The Eveny have different words for wild and domesticated reindeer. A legend of theirs tells how an old hunter, when walking through the forest, came across the head of a reindeer calf protruding from a vulva-shaped crack in the trunk of a larch tree. The old man stroked the calf and talked to it gently, helping it to emerge painfully, one limb at a time until it was fully born. This was the first male reindeer. When this reindeer was three years old it met a female (presumably born from another larch tree) and they had a family of two calves. One day the family was attacked by wolves. The parents cried helplessly to the god Hövki in the sky, while their calves fought back and impaled the wolves on their antlers.

The story continues and ends by explaining why wild and domestic reindeer have gone their separate ways.

For ever after, the reindeer who were born wild stayed wild; but for those who were born with human help, there was no going back.

Vitebsky also recounted how Tolya, his first Eveny friend, learned from Elders of his tribe that reindeer were created by the sky god Hövki, not only to provide food and transport on earth but also to lift the human soul up to the sun.

In a thoroughly researched report, Enn Ernits collected 29 folktales from the Sámi People of the Kola Peninsula in north-western Russia. They are about the mythic reindeer Meandash. The majority of the stories tell of marriages of daughters to reindeer and the subsequent lives of them and their children. A few involve encounters with magic reindeer or the Thunder God or the Sun God.

Anne Ollila shared this origin story from Finland: In Lappish[3] tales reindeer are called the livestock of the Sun. The Sun has given them to people so that they would not have to perish in the fruitless emptiness of the mountains. According to the old Sámi tales, Jubmel created the lands from a reindeer calf. The rocks were created from the bones, the land and soil from its muscles, but the Creator hid the calf's heart deep in the soil. While walking in the wind, a lonely traveller can sometimes hear the heartbeat of a small reindeer calf.

3　The Sámi people of Norway and Sweden never use the term "Lapland[er]" about their region or culture. In Finland it is the common term for the region and the people.

CHAPTER 4

The Santa Story and Rudolph's Nose

Fully domesticated reindeer appear in parades in many countries. Most of these take place during the Christmas season, but the famous one put on by Macy's department store in New York City has reindeer pulling wheeled sleds and people dressed up in the red and white of Santa. It takes place on American Thanksgiving Day, the fourth Thursday of November. To me that is not really a Christmas event, but given the fact that stores start to stock Christmas goods right after Halloween, perhaps we have been "trained" to think it is.

Of course, the reindeer events and stories tied to Christmas would not be complete without Rudolph and his red nose.

There are times and places when Rudolph's avatar appears in cartoons or animated movies as some creature that is not a reindeer. For instance, a red deer fawn or a white-tailed deer (North America), or even, in a streetside sculpture in the town of San Martín de los Andes in Argentina, as a prancing red deer.

My friend Nick Tyler tells me that he once saw a Christmas card in which the "reindeer" was in fact a Uganda kob!

Then there is the famous song about his red nose. "Rudolph the Red-Nosed Reindeer" almost certainly ranks with "Happy Birthday" and "I'm Dreaming of a White Christmas" as one of the most popular and frequently sung songs in the English-speaking world.

It evolved from an 1823 anonymously published poem called "A Visit from St. Nicholas." Readers may be distressed to learn there is no mention of Rudolph in the original. The newer version of the song became a massive hit after it aired in 1964 on the NBC network in a stop-motion, animated TV special under the same name. It has been shown every year and is the longest-running Christmas special of all time. The song itself has been recorded by dozens of artists. Bing Crosby's rendition tops them all, but my favourite is Elvis Presley's.

So what is with the red nose thing in that famous song?

It has to do with the winter coat that has two layers. The inner one is a dense woolly undercoat. Each hair of the outer one is hollow and air-filled, so their bodies are incredibly well insulated. They can withstand temperatures below minus 30ºC. Problems arise when they have to run. They rapidly build up body heat, which must be quickly eliminated. It would be analogous to a human wearing a down jacket during a heat wave and sprinting 100 metres.

Dr. Nicholas Tyler (who saw the kob card) of the Arctic University of Norway in Tromsø, which lies three degrees of latitude (180 kilometres) north of the Arctic Circle, has studied reindeer on the island of Svalbard for almost 40 years. Svalbard is over 900 kilometres north of Tromsø, 800 kilometres inside the Arctic Circle.

When Tyler was interviewed for BBC Earth, in the article titled "Why Reindeer Noses Are More Amazing Than You Think," he said the noses "are immensely complicated."

Inside there is an intricate network of blood vessels that act as heat exchangers. These vessels warm the frigid air before it enters the body on the way to the lungs. When they breathe out, the vessels "capture" the heat and water of the body. The warm air is cooled down by 21ºC from around the normal body temperature of 37ºC to about 16ºC before it's vented outside, saving the majority of that heat. In one extraordinary case it went as low as 6ºC — a 31ºC drop.

Tyler explains, "A reindeer can put the whole system into reverse to dump heat…'like when it's running from a wolf.'"

Sometimes major scientific journals are able to get away from the dry language for which they are best known and incorporate good science with humour. In 2012 the prestigious *British Medical Journal* (now just the BMJ) published such an article by Professor Can Ince and his team. They studied the role of the nose in body heat regulation. Right away in the abstract that precedes the full report we know we are in for something different. The article appeared in the 2012 Christmas issue. They wrote:

> These results highlight the intrinsic physiological properties of Rudolph's legendary luminous red nose, which help to protect it from freezing during sleigh rides and to regulate the temperature of the reindeer's brain, factors essential for flying reindeer pulling Santa Claus's sleigh under extreme temperatures.

Accompanying the solid science, Ince and his colleagues added another nice light touch in their summarized conclusions.

> Rudolph's nose is red because it is richly supplied with red blood cells, comprises a highly dense micro-circulation, and is anatomically and physiologically

adapted for reindeer to carry out their flying duties for Santa Claus.

Taking advantage of modern technology, the BMJ folks took things a step further. In a delightful YouTube video, there is a serious discussion of the medical importance of blood supply in cases of sepsis. We see a tame reindeer being led, just like a well-trained dog at heel, through a passage, past various bits of expensive-looking research equipment to a treadmill where its halter is clipped to a ring. The treadmill starts and the story of the blood supply unfolds. After the animal has been on a treadmill for a short while, a red glow around the nose appears. A photo taken with a thermo-vision camera that scans with infrared radiation (which is not visible to humans) shows the hot areas (yellow is hotter, blue colder). The red has nothing to do with the actual real colour of the nose in daylight. It is just an indication of heat.

The noses of real reindeer — unlike Rudolph's — are not red. The skin is hair-covered and either white or gray.

Another unusual Rudolph story comes from the archives of BBC radio. In a tongue-in-cheek June 2019 online *Mailchimp* article titled "Rudolph the Red Knows Undersea Warfare, Dear," Dan Lewis summarized the report of an unusual and unlikely gift by a Russian general to the Royal Navy captain, Commander Geoffrey Sladen, of the submarine HMS *Trident*. At the time the two countries were allies. In 1941 the sub was patrolling in Scandinavian waters that were mainly the domain of the Russians who were worried about the potential of the Nazis to blockade their seaports.

The British sailors had spent six weeks aboard without supplies and were due to set off on another similar tour. In a delightful, largely symbolic gesture, the Soviets gave them a reindeer. An actual live reindeer.

The question is why. Bill Sainsbury, a Royal Navy Submarine Museum spokesperson, explained the prevailing theory in that radio interview.

> The story goes that the British captain had mentioned his wife had trouble pushing her pram through the snow in England — and the Russian admiral said, "What you need is a reindeer!" And I suppose because it was a gift, they didn't want to seem rude by refusing it.

The reindeer was not called Rudolph, despite the name coined by Lewis in his title. The British crew named her Pollyanna. The challenge was how to get her aboard. She was a small calf, so the problem was soon solved. The ingenious solution was to move her through a torpedo tube.

Pollyanna quickly adapted to her new surroundings. She soon ate all of the moss (the correct food for reindeer) that the Russians had supplied. The men then fed her kitchen scraps and condensed milk that she chose to supplement with navigation charts. Another of her choices was to sleep beside Captain Sladen's bed.

Furthermore, in a delightful BBC blog post titled *Royal Navy Reindeer Submariner's Starring Role on BBC's The One Show*, the archivist of the National Museum of the Royal Navy, George Malcolmson, said, "She would be the first to trot into the control room to be ready for the main hatch to open and the fresh air to pour in. On diving she would go back to her resting area."

After that six-week journey, Pollyanna had grown too big to exit the way she had come in. Eventually, she was trussed and removed, as Lewis wrote, by being "finessed out of the main hatch."

She did not return to the sea. She was moved to the Regent's Park zoo (now called the London Zoo) where she soon became a firm favourite. In that BBC radio *The One Show* report, "It was rumoured that she never forgot her submarine career for whenever she heard bells or a sound like a submarine tannoy she would lower her head as though preparing for diving stations."

She died in 1947, the same year the *Trident* was broken up for scrap.

CHAPTER 5

Caribou in Canada

My foray into caribou research came as a nice surprise. I'd been working on a moose project near the town of Rochester in Alberta where I'd joined broad-shouldered, tough-as-nails Randy Frojker, then later Bill Mytton with his Abe Lincoln beard, and lanky Tom Hauge, as they studied several aspects of the biology of the largest deer in the world.

We put on radio collars and collected blood samples for disease studies and hormone levels. We also took all kinds of body measurements. Videos on my website show moose captures involving a calculated dose of immobilizing drug that allowed us to lead animals out of thick forest into clearings where we collected samples and weighed them. To get the weight, we cobbled together a sling made from some old collars, ropes and poles cut from nearby trees hooked up to a scale suspended from the underside of the helicopter.

It's handy when memories come back at the right moment. The "walking with moose" idea came directly from the experience of pulling sedated two-ton elephant youngsters into transport crates during a project in Rwanda.

With great skill, the helicopter pilot drove the huge animals towards us. He went slowly, moving from side to side to balance their movements and ensure they reached us exactly at the ambush site that had been chosen. Then they were darted with the right dose, based upon their size, to allow us to keep them standing so we could place ropes on legs. A large crew of locals joined the team as we dragged the woozy animals to the crates.

We even moved a few of the very young in slings, although there was no scale involved. Once back at camp we could give the calves the antidote to wake them from their stupor.

At first glance, these techniques may not seem to have anything to do with studies of caribou that began five years later in Canada.

When he saw us walking the moose and heard the elephant story, Tom asked if I would help with his caribou work. He was trying to collect the same moose data set we had obtained from a boreal forest population in the Birch Mountains north of Fort McKay, which lies 500 kilometres north of Edmonton, Alberta's capital city (see the map of the Birch Mountains in the photo section). Over an evening beer, he said, "I'm running into a few problems with this study. Too many are succumbing to the effects of the capture."

It sounded to me like a stress situation. If run, or even handled, too hard, too fast or for too long, animals (including humans) may die very quickly, or after a few hours or days or an even longer period due to extensive muscle and other organ damage. The condition is commonly known as *capture myopathy*. I could not tell for sure.

We started on the caribou work by darting them from a helicopter, the capture method that Tom had been using. It was at once obvious to me that these animals, as the saying goes, were "a horse of another colour."

Where moose run from a buzzing helicopter in a straight line that makes darting a doddle, caribou make a top-class rugby winger three quarter or a Canadian/American football running back look like a slouch. As soon as the machine got as close as 10 or 15 metres, they either jinked under or turned away from the machine at full speed. Our pilot, Fred Wiskar, his dark hair swept back to the right, when working with us always wearing a jean jacket, used all of his considerable skill to help us, but it was no use. We simply could not get a decent shot in less than the self-imposed two minutes that I considered the maximum allowable to prevent capture myopathy.

We managed to get only one caribou in two hours of flying — a very costly rate of return. After wasting four darts that were buried in the ground instead of the rump of the target, I suggested a new plan.

The transfer of experiences with elephants proved to be the solution. When we saw a group of caribou, we dropped down-wind near some trees where I could hide and wait for action. The terrain consisted mostly of small stands of stunted spruce interspersed with a variety of woody shrubs.

It was my task to hide in a suitable clump, dart gun at the ready, in the hope that Fred could maneuver the herd past me within a 40-metre range at a walk. In all such wildlife capture endeavours the key person is the pilot. Fred soon figured out the precise distance, speed and altitude needed. It was like watching a champion border collie move a reluctant flock of sheep into a small pen.

My job was relatively easy. All I had to do was follow the shooting range routine at the right moment. Ready, aim, fire.

We didn't have a two-way radio with us but a signal after a good shot was to step away from cover and raise my arms. The chopper headed off to watch the animal until it succumbed to the effect of the drugs. Tom and John Jorgensen, the tousle-haired technician on the project, would hop off to tend to the patient while Fred picked me up from my stand.

A couple of times, when the animal did not oblige by going and staying down, we had to use the "walking with caribou" (or elephant or moose) technique to extricate it from heavier patches of bush. With all of us working it took little time, no more than 10 or 15 minutes, to collect blood samples, pluck some hair for analysis and take body measurements.

With the collar in place, it was easy to lift the caribou onto a crude pallet made from lengths of poplar, tie it down for safety and hoist it under the hovering machine to which a scale was attached. Now it was time to call out the checklist to make sure we hadn't forgotten a key step.

Then came the administration of the antidote. Within a minute the caribou was on its feet. After a quick shake and a look around it headed off into the trees.

After a couple of slower sessions, as the team learned the ropes, we had steady success.

The collar served double duty. The bright colours, often a combination of blue and white, made it easy to see in the heavy wooded areas. Its radio signal would transmit to the receiver in the chopper.

From Alberta I moved to my home province and joined biologist Jim Rettie, who was also studying boreal forest reindeer. We used the more satisfactory ambush method, even when the temperature dropped to well below zero. The challenge was to keep the gun, and my hands, warm. The hands issue was easily dealt with — a good pair of mitts. The gun was trickier. It had to stay above freezing because I'd learned, during those earlier moose projects, that Saskatchewan's minus 20 in January is not the same as the plus-20 conditions on the equator. In the cold, hands rapidly chill on the gun barrel and fluid in the darts freezes in short order. The dart in the barrel goes the same way. For some reason a dart filled with a block of ice doesn't work as it might. The solution? Carry the gun in its case, alongside a hot water bottle. Pull it out at the last minute and put it back as soon as possible. We used the same techniques but had to do more of the walking to clearings because of the greater number and height of the trees. This time we used a net for the lifting and weighing.

Since then, of course, the collars have become so sophisticated, with GPS and other data transmission, even heart rate, that they can relay everything needed back to base. One hardly needs the helicopter to follow the animal after the initial capture. Drone use has allowed less invasive, much less expensive and longer lasting observation.

In the late 1970s, a New Zealand invention completely changed the entire capture, research and translocation of animals all over the world. It started as a hand-held net gun that was fired from the chopper to drop the net just ahead of the fleeing target — in the case of New Zealand, red deer.

Entrepreneur extraordinaire, deer farmer and go-getter Tim Wallis, later Sir Tim, explained the method. "We have developed the method so that a weight is attached to each corner of a big net. The weights are inserted into each of four barrels located at the corners of a fibreglass basket." It was no hardship to take up his invitation for a demonstration in one of his deer paddocks.

The process was both impressive and simple. Tim flew up behind a young stag. John Muir, beside him, the passenger door back at base, was the shooter. Without a word spoken by either man, he fired at exactly the right moment. The net blossomed out in an arc, spread out and enveloped the animal. John jumped out of the machine and quickly hog-tied the deer. He was so fast I didn't catch up until the leather straps were all buckled. The net came off in double-quick time. This was a team as well tuned as a concert-ready grand piano. Because this was just a demo case for my benefit, he untied the deer. It leapt to its feet, no doubt surprised at the whole process, and shot off across the field. "Of course," Tim explained. "It can be collared or moved as fits the situation."

Wallis took the process to the next logical step. He arranged that two nets be mounted on the machine. His technical staff linked the charges on the basket to switches on the cyclic stick (often misnamed "joystick") controlled by him. This meant any pilot had complete control and could fire the charges at the right moment. If he missed with the first effort, he could fire again or capture two animals in one run.

In the United States, from the 1980s, the method, initially using the triangular net on coyotes, has been used for hundreds of animals of many species. The much better four-barrel soon followed.

Since then, many other creatures have been studied or translocated after net gun capture. They include wild sheep, deer of several species from mule deer to moose, coyotes, wetland birds, even eagles. In Africa many scientists have also extensively used the four-barrel set-up. For instance, my friend and fellow wildlife vet Dr. Pete Morkel of Namibia has used it on 18 African species that include the hippo. (Only young hippo, of course.) He did mention that their parents were not overly impressed and on the odd occasion he and his colleagues had to decamp at speed.

For a short while the skid-mounted four-barrel was used in the United States, but discussions with government agencies, no doubt involving the "illegal modification of an air frame," have meant that the use of skid-mounted net guns has been discontinued.

However, no capture system is 100 per cent safe or perfect. In one of our many email exchanges, Dr. Morkel wrote: "It's a great piece of equipment if used on the right animals in the right situation and it's an equally lethal piece of equipment (for man and beast!), if used wrongly." The major cause of mortality among the target animals is neck fracture. There have also been some human deaths related to the risks involved.

Caribou net gun capture is safer, quicker and less costly than any darting system. Since 2019 it has been the only method employed for caribou translocation or research work in Canada.

CHAPTER 6

A Visit to Finland

In 1988 the American Association of Zoo Veterinarians (AAZV) chose Toronto as the venue for its annual conference. I had been a member since arriving in Canada in 1975, so this gathering of like-minded souls was a basic requirement for both my professional life and enjoyment of meeting old friends and colleagues and making new ones.

The conference is a serious scientific gathering. Folks working in the five main disciplines of zoological medicine gather to exchange ideas and learn new techniques. We learn about events in the fields of zoo medicine, free-ranging wildlife, reptiles and amphibians, marine mammals and birds. Those are in the formal sessions. At least as much exchange occurs over coffee and other breaks. Even over dinner and the odd tipple.

Imagine, then, the extraordinary opening to one of the presentations. The MC introduced a mop-haired Dr. Harry Jalanka, scraggy beard and all. His lilting accent confirmed him to be from Finland, as we all knew from the printed program. His first slide appeared on the screen. We saw a small furry creature in the background of the title words, "Management of Norwegian Lemmings *Lemmus lemmus* at Helsinki Zoo."

Like most of my 200-odd colleagues, I knew the myth about herds of lemmings charging over cliffs to their death. I didn't know much else except that the little creatures are rodents. This sounded exactly like what we were hoping for. New information about a species we knew little about.

Then Dr. Jalanka opened his talk. Not with formal words as one might expect in such a gathering but with a phrase we all knew well from our kindergarten storytelling days: "Once upon a time, in the frozen far north of Norway..."

There may have been one or two fuddy-duddies who were insulted at such levity, but not most of us. We learned a whole lot and I enjoyed the talk. It struck me that Harry was presenting (performing?) in his third language. That takes some guts.

Finland is a bilingual country. Finnish and Swedish share more or less equal time. He was in Canada showing us that he was a sound clinician with a sense of humour.

During the morning coffee break, Harry and I found ourselves standing next to a table covered in several different textbooks on veterinary medicine. Before long we had struck up an animated conversation. We both had experience with northern creatures. There were free-ranging moose in Finland and a display of them at Helsinki's Korkeasaari Zoo. I had radio-collared a bunch of them in Canada. I had also joined a research team working on caribou. Reindeer are an important part of the ancient culture of Finnish people. Beer and good food were other common interests. We met again in 1988 at the AAZV meeting in Greensboro, North Carolina, and shared some laughs and a good time (as well, of course, as paying close attention to the science). I quizzed him about the reindeer industry and learned a bit about it, but he told me he didn't work with them as much as some of his colleagues who were more familiar with the subject. That stayed in my mind as tasty bait.

By this time in my career I had developed a keen interest in the ways that humans use wildlife as farmed and ranched animals. Not just in general. On my first trip to New Zealand, my wife Jo and I had seen the impressive development of the deer farming industry. The deer were mainly red deer, but a few fallow deer farms had also started up. We had been there again, and I had spent three months conducting breeding research all over both islands. There were also a few elk farms in my home Canadian province of Saskatchewan.

With red and fallow deer, as well as elk, farming in my mental library, there was one thing missing. I knew that worldwide there were more reindeer being used in extensive ranching than all other deer species combined. Naturally, the reindeer of Scandinavia, especially those of the Sámi People of Norway, Sweden and neighbouring Finland, were the ones I had read and heard most about. I discovered there are over a million domesticated reindeer in Russia. But I knew nothing more. Management techniques, nutrition, breeding strategies, handling and diseases: all were no more than guesswork.

One of the perks of a university post was the option to apply for a sabbatical every seventh year. Not just an opportunity to head off to a sun-drenched beach. An application required a written proposal of work to be done and possible outcomes that would be of benefit to the institution. In 1990 I knew that next year I was eligible. The application went up the ladder to the dean. The plan was to visit countries where deer farming, or ranching, was being carried out and to learn more about the details of the various enterprises. Approval was soon in place.

Now it was time to refine an itinerary. Scandinavia was the obvious starting point. Not only did both Jo and I have family in Europe — mine in England, hers in Holland, so we could start with visits to both — but Holland was a natural jumping-off point to Sweden and then Finland, where I could catch up with Harry and meet his reindeer-wise colleagues.

We set off by car, kindly loaned by Geraldine, Jo's sister, from Apeldoorn, in early September. North through Germany, into Denmark. At the Copenhagen Zoo we saw our first ever reindeer, which, of course, looked exactly like the caribou at home. Then, after some tourist stuff around interesting historical buildings, we headed to Helsingør. As we are dedicated theatregoers, the 16th-century Kronborg castle was on our bucket list. With the name change to Elsinore, Shakespeare's famous tragedy *Hamlet, Prince of Denmark* is set there. Indeed, many famous actors have performed on the grounds over the years.

Then we boarded the ferry for the half-hour ride to Helsingborg in Sweden across the narrow channel that divides the two countries.

After a five-hour drive north of the ferry terminal, we stopped in Kolmården to visit another wildlife vet, Dr. Bengt Ole-Röken and his wife Barbro for a couple of nights on our way north. Bengt, a tall, solidly built blond who fits the TV image of a typical Swede, is another vet I had met several times at those AAZV gatherings.

A group of a dozen reindeer occupied a large enclosure. There were five half-grown calves, their antlers in velvet peeking up from their skulls. Six adult cows, four with thin antlers from 30 to 40 centimetres long, two just spikes, the others antlerless. The star was a full-grown bull with multi-branched antlers curving forward, reaching way up, at least as long as he was tall.

We had two other firsts. Before a sumptuous dinner featuring roast wild boar, we had our first experience of a sauna at their home. Hot, steamy, not madly refreshing, but certainly sweat-inducing. It seemed to come from every pore, even ones I didn't know I had. A cascade of the stuff poured off my bald pate into my eyes. A first that would never be forgotten. For Scandinavians the sauna is a matter of course. It's even a verb.

By lunchtime next morning we were in Stockholm where we met briefly with Harry who was at a conference. We agreed to meet for the evening, so Jo and I had an enjoyable time touring the beautiful old city.

Next day we joined Harry on his return to Helsinki, travelling by ferry overnight across the Baltic, for a while gazing in wonder at the star-filled sky with no light pollution to obscure the view.

For the three nights we stayed in Finland's capital Harry had arranged for us to use the apartment owned by the zoo. It was fully equipped with linen, dishes and everything else to make us comfortable.

Jo went with Christina, Harry's slim, blond wife, for some coffee and visiting. We all gathered that evening for a very Finnish dinner. September is the peak of the mushroom harvest. Our starter, ordered ahead by Harry, consisted of two bowls of soup, each made from a different kind of wild mushroom. Two more memorable firsts.

Next morning I went with him to the zoo where we worked on a couple of cases, including checking a lame reindeer. I was getting warmer in my quest to see how they are managed and behave. It was at once obvious from both zoo visits that their temperament is radically different than the caribou of the Forestry Farm Zoo in Saskatoon. Harry told me that the zoo had managed reindeer for many years. The breeding program was so successful that the zoo regularly supplied other institutions with stock.

The following day, I again crossed in the little ferry to the zoo, which was located on an island only accessible by boat. We spent the whole day working on more cases. The most memorable of these was a tiger that Harry anaesthetized before we entered the pen. A stunning experience. I had worked on plenty of lions in

Africa, but this beautiful creature was quite a bit bigger. The head and mouth were much the same as my former patients, but the stripes made a big impression. I couldn't resist running my hand over its body. The muscles were solid and the coat had the same rough feel as those of lions. It remains the only one I have ever been close to or worked on.

As far as getting closer to the actual reindeer studies was concerned, Harry gave us the perfect contact. He phoned Mauri Nieminen at his office in the town of Rovaniemi, just six kilometres north of the Arctic Circle, some 800 kilometres north of Helsinki (see the map of Finland in the photo section). We were in luck.

Mauri, who was head of the Reindeer Research Program of the Game and Fisheries Research Institute, was the lead researcher in the field. He was heading to the northernmost research station in the country after the weekend. We would be welcome to join him.

This was even more of a bonus because it meant that Harry and Christina could manage a couple of days off and take us to a cabin on the Baltic shore near the town of Turku for a wonderful weekend of relaxation and fishing, as well as, of course, a sauna. The wind was way too strong for us to go out in the rented boat, but the supper of trout (purchased locally), a delicate Chardonnay and good cheer round the log fire was not exactly unpleasant.

On the Monday we headed north.

As we headed to Rovaniemi, we realized that most of the northern region of Finland is reindeer country. Road hazard signs made that obvious. In no time at all we saw a group of deer on the road. They stopped to take a look, as if they knew they had the right of way. We later learned this wasn't necessarily true; they are frequently the cause of traffic accidents.

We met solidly built Mauri, his neatly trimmed beard and dark hair beneath a matching black Breton cap, at his office in town. With him was a young, tall, blond Nordic vet, Dr. Timo Soveri, who explained that he was researching the efficacy and safety of Ivermectin, a potentially important deworming drug for reindeer.

We were soon off to our final destination near the community of Kaamanen, a further 300 kilometres north. It is near the village of Kutuharju where Mauri had been conducting several studies.

The journey provided an extra treat. We had arrived at exactly the right time to see the beautiful autumn colours known as *ruska* of the trees, shrubs and plants of northern Finland. They range from the yellow of the birches, through the oranges and reds of the shrubs, the purple of the blueberries and the brown, pale blue, green and white of the lichens that are one of the main feed items for the deer. Tourists visit in droves at this time of year just for the magical sight.

It was at Kutuharju for the first time that I'd ever seen large numbers of the reindeer being herded and handled. They were way easier to deal with than beef cattle, not much more so than dairy cows. The herdsmen had no trouble drafting some and then gently pushing them, one at a time, through the door of the shed where we were working. Sample collection was simple. We lifted each deer onto a canvas sheet covering a rough wooden frame nailed against the wall. A cushioned board, hinged above and some 40 centimetres wide, was flipped down across its back. A short length of rope tied to the buckle of an old leather belt attached to the back of the cushion was at once tightened to the frame under the deer's belly. While one man held the head, the deer did not struggle as Timo collected his samples.

With the work all done, we headed to the wooden cabin where we would spend the night. Before the evening meal, Mauri suggested we go and pick some cloudberries. The pale golden berries, growing low to the ground on woody shrubs, have small bobbles just like a blackberry. We had never even heard of them, but they turned out to be delicious. Many vanished into our mouths before we reached the cabin.

For supper we were treated to a traditional Finnish meal: chopped reindeer meat stewed in a big stainless-steel pot, plus yellow Finnish potatoes with their slightly nutty flavour. It was okay, but I would very much have preferred a tender steak.

The cabin wasn't insulated in any way, so the sleeping bags we had in our backpacks, rated to minus 10, were only just warm enough, even with the hood up and knotted under the chin. A sweater and pants made the difference.

I woke to the sound of someone trying to start a chainsaw. The windows seemed to be rattling. Shortly, my sleep-befuddled brain told me that the loud noise was not machine-derived. It was Mauri's snores shaking the windows and reverberating round the room. I reckon he could have snored for Finland, if not for Europe. There was no way I was going to get back to sleep. A trip to the truck parked by the door didn't help, as it was far too cold out there, so I shivered back to my wooden bunk and tried to drown the noise with layers of hat, sweater and coat.

CHAPTER 7

Finland's Reindeer Industry

We left Kaamanen after a simple cereal breakfast and headed south to the town of Inari, where we stopped at an official reindeer slaughter plant. Inside the set-up was like most such places but with an interesting difference. Instead of hanging on over-head hooks, the carcasses lay horizontally on a rack, where men dressed in white processed them with speed and efficiency.

Mauri explained that this was one of the very few modern slaughter plants with meat-cutting facilities approved by government. Field slaughter was being phased out and there would be more plants built in the near future to cater to the needs of the industry.

Then it was another 30-minute drive to Ivalo, where Timo boarded a plane in order to get his precious samples back to the lab in good shape. Just south of the town Mauri stopped to show us some wooden racks covered in dried plant material that looked, from a distance, like hay. A closer look showed it was obviously not hay in the sense of being dried grass. It was what I know as mare's tail (*Equisetum*), easily recognized by its central fleshy stem and numerous small radiating tendrils at each node.

It seems to grow in many parts of the world. I know it as part of the natural winter diet of caribou in some regions of Canada. For other folks it is a popular garden plant where there is lots of moisture. For others yet, it is a weed, a pest. For the latter it is to be poisoned, routed and rooted out as quickly as possible before it takes over the garden. Mauri explained that it is important because it's a source of winter feed for the deer.

Then it was on to Rovaniemi. For the next four hours I woke every now and again from the inevitable after-effects of the sleep-deprived, snore-infused night at the reindeer research station.

We stayed there for two nights and enjoyed our walks around the town, spending most of one morning at the Santa Claus village. Finns have promoted the town as the official home of the white-bearded character. Of course, we stopped in at several stores and were particularly entranced with one that carried every imaginable Santa-related item. As if she had been a model advertising the entire inventory, Jo's red raincoat and the traditional Finnish hat she tried on were the perfect fit for the scene. She sat on a pile of stacked hides, finding out they are soft and warm. An attendant told us they are used as attractive rugs, and particularly for the creation of winter jackets. That winter hair also makes a fine mattress.

One of the restaurants in the village served smoked reindeer meat (what else?). The processing was perfect, tasty, tender and not too smoky. We rounded out our unusual meal with cloudberry ice cream. Another tasty first.

That evening we decided to take in a movie. Our 15-year-old son had recommended the Leslie Nielsen comedy, *Naked Gun* 2 ½. It took quite a while to get past the distraction of the screen, its bottom half covered in caption lines translated into two languages, Finnish and Swedish.

The next day Mauri told us he had news for us. A reindeer roundup and field slaughter was scheduled near the town of Kemijärvi, only an hour's drive east. He had also contacted a vet, Dr. Marjatta Rantalla, who lived there and told us she would meet us at the entrance sign of the town. This was a golden opportunity to learn. Jo and I were packed and on our way within five minutes.

Marjatta met us as expected and we headed off down a rough track. Round a bend only 100 metres from the road a red and white truck, easily identifiable as a mobile refrigerator unit by the air extractor above the cab, was parked beside a fire where a group of men stood warming themselves. For the next two hours we stood and watched, fascinated by the ease and efficiency of the work being done.

We had arrived too late to see the deer being brought into the corral. "Corral" is really too strong a word. Most of the "wall" was made of some green snow fence tied to nearby trees and a length of plastic sheeting. A dozen men, two of them holding a deer, stood chatting inside the pen, while the other animals were bunched together at the other end.

Some females were grabbed by their small antlers, injected with de-wormer and shunted away through a gate, constructed from wooden boards, leading back to the forest. They took little time to head away but soon stopped and stood watching the proceedings.

One female was taken out on a halter and tied to a nearby tree. I asked Marjatta what was going on. "Oh," she replied, "every new calf that is with a female has its ears notched. Each herder has his own marks and every herder knows the other marks. That female belongs to another herder. It must have joined these ones. They have called on their phones and told him about it."

The team leader asked me not to take any photos of the actual slaughter. Marjatta explained that they didn't really know who I was and were concerned I might be some sort of animal rights activist travelling incognito and out to do them damage.

The juvenile males were taken aside behind a sheet of burlap and quickly and efficiently slaughtered. The whole process was fascinating. Instead of hanging the carcass on a hook, they laid it on a specially designed sled and rapidly skinned and gutted it. Then, now clean, it was hoisted into the custom-designed truck.

A curved rail with hooks to hold each deer hung from the roof. The government meat inspector checked each one as it was hoisted into the vehicle. When the rail was full, the overhead door was pulled down and the truck headed off to the central market. The whole process took only an hour.

Marjatta invited us to her home and asked if we could stay for a couple of nights. We at once took her up on the kind offer and followed her back to Kemijärvi. We passed through on the main street and about a kilometre later turned onto a gravel track that curved between a mixed stand of spruce and silver birch trees. She stopped at the end of the track beside a wooden bungalow. Away to the left a small log cabin stood near a lake.

Our bags were no more than a metre inside the front door when she said, "Have you sauna today?"

Before we knew it, we were carrying two white towels over to the log cabin near the lake. We stripped off on the veranda and hung our clothes on hooks by the door. Inside a fire was burning under a metal grid, above which a pile of soccer-ball-sized rocks, encased in a sort of cage, was radiating heat. As we had learned in Sweden, we poured water from a jug over the stones. A cloud of steam at once filled the air, almost obscuring us from each other. My lungs felt as if they were being dragged out through my mouth. Not being hardy Finns, sweat dripping off our bodies, Jo and I abandoned the shed in short order and quickly covered the ten metres to the water, which was nearing its transition stage between liquid and solid form, no more than a couple of degrees above zero. Simultaneous gasps, followed at once by scrotum contraction and nipple hardening, occurred in less than a second. Return to the shore took a teeny bit longer. We were soon dressing back at the cabin.

We returned to the house and met Ollé, Marjatta's husband. Later, after dinner, they showed us a map of the area. The town was on a narrow isthmus in the centre of a large lake system that looks like a three-tentacled octopus on a bad hair day, stretching some 50 kilometres north and south.

Next day we relaxed and explored the area, again marvelling at the colours of the trees and undergrowth.

It was time to move on. After another lunch of delicious smoked reindeer sandwiches in Rovaniemi, we headed north to the border post with Sweden and on to the next leg of our journey, much wiser about the reindeer culture of the Lapland herders.

Part Two

MONGOLIAN

EXPERIENCES

CHAPTER 8

An Unexpected Visit

The first day back at work after any overseas trip is inevitably filled with matters that need immediate attention. The Monday after family visits in Europe in late April 2004 was no exception. As I waded through too many emails, one of which was a request to present a paper in Bangalore the following week about the effects of high pressure on unstable gas mixtures, I needed to start on the replies. There was one dated April 13 from someone named Morgan Keay of the Itgel Foundation. I'd never heard of her or it but decided to open the message anyway. She explained that she wanted to come to Saskatoon "later this week" to discuss reindeer. She wrote, "The Itgel Foundation is committed to protecting the Tsaatan People's cultural legacy by working to restore the health, numbers, and sustainability of their interdependent reindeer herd." Her "later this week" was the week before.

I was wondering about this when my graduate student Dr. Murray Woodbury knocked and stuck his head round the door. "A woman named Morgan Keay is in the buffeteria. She's waiting to see you. She called last week, and I told her you'd be back from holiday today. She says she's driven up from Colorado and arrived this morning."

"Give me a moment to check her email and I'll be right behind you," I said.

There were 30-odd students sitting, chatting, snacking, some with cups or water bottles in hand at the round tables in the buff. Murray, a red-headed young woman with a ponytail, and a guy with a beard were over near the microwaves.

"Hi Jerry, this is Morgan Keay, and over there is Jason Johns. They've driven up from Boulder."

"Hi there," I said as I shook hands. "Excuse me a moment, I'll just get myself a cuppa and a cookie."

Morgan confirmed that she and Jason had indeed driven for some 22 hours up from Colorado, including a brief camping stop overnight.

"What keeps you in Boulder?" I asked.

"I was at university there and now I'm the executive director of the Boulder Symphony Orchestra. It's not a year-round job, so I work in Mongolia in the off-season."

By now I'd read, and reread, the email. Morgan was not just *with* the foundation. She was the executive director after co-founding it.

As we sat over our hot drinks she gave me a brief summary about Itgel.

"Liliana Goldman and I founded the organization after we spent several months in the country. We supported some local initiatives but only at the request of the people. I wonder if you have time to get involved with the reindeer project."

"Tell me more," I said. "What's the project about?"

"It's all about reindeer, which is why we're here. Lil and I went to Mongolia on a university student program with the School for International Training and lived with different families who spoke no English. By the end I had learned enough Mongolian to do some travelling.

"I went to the northwest, to a village called Tsagaan Nuur that lies in the Darkhad Valley. It's the administrative centre (*soum*) of the *aimag* (equivalent of a Canadian province) of Hovsgol, and lies in the foothills of the Sayan Mountains. It was there that I met families of the ancient nomadic reindeer herding culture known as the Tsaatan or Dukha who have their reindeer in the mountains. They ride them and milk them. The animals just stick around, often hanging out near camp as if they haven't a care in the world.

"Most residents in Tsagaan Nuur are Darkhad (the valley was named for them), but there are some Tsaatan who live there and many of their children come down from the mountains for their schooling. It's the starting point for the journey into the mountains where the herders have their reindeer. When I was there, they asked for help with disease and breeding problems. The reindeer herd numbers are way down and that's a concern as well. That's why I'm here."

"How come the numbers dropped?" I asked.

She continued, "The reason reindeer numbers have declined goes back to the time when the Russians enforced the border with People's Republic of Mongolia in the 1920s and took over the admin. The traditional herders were forced into collectiviz-ation programs and made to leave the mountains and work in community centres like Tsagaan Nuur. Then, in 1984, Perestroika came, and the Russian domination ended when the communist party in Mongolia collapsed. By 1992 the Russians no longer had a role there. Many herders returned to their traditional way of life. By then the herd numbers had dropped sharply from what was estimated to have been 3,000 head to under a thousand, perhaps as few as 700.

"They're ethnically Tuvan. Most members of the culture live across the border in Russia. But the border is strictly controlled, and they can't cross. In fact, one group of hunters was caught on the wrong side by Russian guards and held for a month before being released back home. They once spoke Tuvan, but very few folks on the Mongolian side can still do so."

She'd been in touch with Norm Mitchell, one of my reindeer clients. He told her about my work in New Zealand and the pioneering of artificial insemination (AI) of red deer in the commercial herds there. Morgan knew about my book about managing farmed deer but was obviously probing a bit deeper. What experience did I have? Did I have any reindeer clients? What did I know about reindeer diseases?

I was in a position to deal with all three of her questions. The experience thing was easy. I had worked on several different deer species, including domestic reindeer and their wild caribou cousins here in North America, for over 25 years. The vet college's clinical department, of which I was a member, had several reindeer clients in the province, scattered at varying distances from the city. One client lived barely ten kilometres from the college, and I had visited his farm with a group of students just before we'd left for Europe.

I told her, "One of the farms we've been to belongs to Mr. Mitchell, the guy you contacted. My students were amazed to be able to take a couple of calves and a quiet cow for a walk down the road below his house just last fall. The calves had never had a halter on them before, but it was just like taking a dog for a walk. Easy. I even took some photos of them. He said he was training them for the Christmas parades that he does every year."

"As I said," she replied, "I've been talking to him about one of the problems in Mongolia. The herders have asked me to find out · if artificial insemination can be done because they are worried about inbreeding as most of the bulls are closely related to one another. Norman has collected semen from one of his bulls and we have been asked by the herders to see if we can organize some artificial insemination to bring in new blood."

I replied that I'd done quite a lot of research on artificial insemination and had success with it in New Zealand red deer, elk and white-tailed deer here at the zoo.

"As for diseases," I said, "there's a nasty condition called brucellosis. It's the major one in caribou here and, with the exception of Norway, Sweden and Finland, it occurs in more eastern regions of Eurasia. It causes arthritis and abortion among other things. Caribou have their own *Brucella* species, different than the cattle and goat ones."

"Yes, I know," she replied. "One of the Tsaatan veterinary technicians has a close personal connection with it. His wife is so sick she can barely function. Her arthritis is severe, and she is in constant pain."

Brucellosis has also hit home in my own family. One of my aunts, who lived on a farm and drank unpasteurized milk all her life, got infected with it. She had three miscarriages and one tiny little girl, who lived less than a day. Her other two children, my cousins Fran and Jonathan, are alive and well.

Our conversation lasted way longer than a coffee break and we ended up talking our way through lunch. The chance to work in such an interesting environment, with the world's most intriguing domestic animal and yet another culture, was too good to miss. It would involve disease study, and the chance to provide useful experience on artificial breeding based on my own successes with three other deer species. It also offered a golden opportunity to expand what I had learned in Finland and at home. Just the fact that the Tsaatan milk their reindeer was amazing.

I guess I passed her scrutiny. She asked me if I would be interested in going to Mongolia to work with the team. I hesitated no more than a nanosecond.

"I'll have to see if I can secure some funding," she said. "When might you be free?"

"Would September work?" I asked.

"I'll be back to you, but it sounds ideal."

Morgan and Jason headed out on their long trip back to Colorado and within a week a detailed email appeared. It outlined more about the challenges involved. Then on my birthday in June came a formal invitation and a request to contact a travel agent in Toronto who deals with Itgel matters.

Inevitably, Morgan and I exchanged a flurry of emails across the aether.

CHAPTER 9

Off to Mongolia

Apart from the travel papers and tickets, there were two things to worry about: clothes and equipment. Nothing fancy in the wardrobe line. Just one lot of something respectable would suit. The rest was simple. I had enough fieldwork under my belt to be able to pack for almost any conditions. Arctic, rainforest, desert, even comfortable temperate. Good rain gear was a must and for this trip tough trousers for horse riding.

The veterinary component had two elements. First, syringes, needles, blood collection equipment, emergency surgical kit, stethoscope and thermometer. Second, for the humans, a first-aid package and antibiotics in case of some sort of infection. All that was easy.

Most important was to find a way to test for brucellosis. The only way to do so under field conditions is to use a special card called a Brewer diagnostic card that has little pear-shaped windows. Into each is put two tiny drops of serum that are then mixed with a special purple stain.

There is an important limitation. The test has to be carried out in a draught-proof place and at a temperature close to 21ºC. I'd no idea if those requirements could be met.

An application to get the kits proved to be something of a bureaucratic nightmare. They weren't available in Canada. I had to get them from a United States government source, but only if I went through Canada Agriculture channels. Inevitably, the bureaucrats did what bureaucrats tend to do best, so things took a long time to happen.

Eventually, the happening happened, but only after many phone calls, letters, form filling and the loss of several dozen more hairs from the top of my already sparse pate.

Finally came a late August departure. With tickets, visas and other paperwork in hand, I headed out for what would be a tough journey. Saskatoon — Vancouver — Beijing to start. Then Ulaanbaatar. With a long wait in Vancouver, and the trans-Pacific leg, I was exhausted by the time I arrived. Jetlag does that to me, more so if I'm westbound than east.

To add to that was the nightmarish bureaucracy of the Chinese immigration system. Reams of paper, endless lineups. The first bottleneck, even before any passengers got to the immigration kiosks, was at a station where we all passed through a body temperature scanner. I suppose that any passengers whose temperature exceeded a pre-set maximum would be pulled aside and quarantined. I have no idea how it works, but this was very soon after the SARS outbreak that affected so many Chinese people and spread to Canada. Indeed, it reached into my own family when our grandson Mathew was born. He was delivered in Toronto and nobody was allowed to visit the ward to see him and his mother — not even Magda's mother who had flown in from Poland especially for the big event. It must have been very tough on her as she had virtually no English and was stuck all day in a tiny flat while Charles, her son-in-law, went off to his medical research lab.

These sorts of lineups are not much fun when you are fresh. They are tiresome when you are already three parts on the way to zombiehood. The whole experience was sadly not exhausting enough to induce a sound sleep at the hotel. Next morning it was back to the airport. If the arrival had been confusing, the departure was almost beyond belief. Endless lineups and crowds that made Heathrow look like a deserted shopping mall at midnight. I finally sat to grab some rest when I spotted a copy of the local English *China Daily News* and browsed through it. I jerked from mild curiosity to full interest in a split second. An article described how a local man had been arrested because he added cat urine to a beef dish at his restaurant in order to make it seem as if it was tiger meat. Tiger bones and other products are a vital part of Chinese traditional medicine.

Finally, the boarding for Ulaanbaatar, or UB as the guy in the next seat told me.

This time, with Morgan's official letter of invitation in hand, the passage through immigration and customs was a cakewalk. Neither my backpack nor my huge blue and gray CCM hockey bag, filled with clothes, sleeping bag and an array of veterinary equipment, elicited any interest.

Jason, still bearded, was right at the exit. What a relief! We were soon installed in a small rattletrap of a taxi. The most intriguing thing was the length of blue silk-like material draped around the rear-view mirror. "That's a good luck item," explained Jason. "Most Mongolians are Buddhists and blue is the most important colour. You will see it all over the place."

The drive into the city was an eye-opener. There was a lineup at a toll gate. We hardly slowed, moving faster than expected. It was at once easy to figure out why. The booths were empty, the concrete crumbling. On our left stood an industrial complex with smoke from a tall chimney belching into the sky. A meandering gravel-bedded river tumbled along beside it.

I couldn't help examining each ripple to imagine where a trout might lie but decided that the factory and city would probably have driven any of them away, even if they had been there in former times.

Soon came the outskirts. Numerous small wooden houses, many of them brightly painted, were crowded together. Each house had its little patch demarcated by a wooden fence.

We soon got into the old part of town. For the first few kilometres UB is a mass of concrete high-rises, each one a clone of the other. The murals on the ends of the buildings, with chunky, grim-looking figures glaring out, looked like leftover communist images from the Stalin era, the paint well worn and patchy. Not the beauty of Vienna or Venice.

We crossed an iron bridge and, although the concrete apartment blocks were still around us, there were plenty of other interesting buildings. On our left, just after the bridge, was a fenced-in garden. The unkempt collection of grass and weeds partly obscured a multi-roofed, decorated building. It looked like the ornate temples one sees in pictures of China.

We swung left onto a main thoroughfare, called Peace Avenue, where Jason pointed out the post office. "That's where we can call home. It's our only means of communication. They have a good bank of phones and there are usually open lines." He pointed, "The apartment is a few blocks up there."

We dragged my gear up a couple of flights of worn concrete steps to the rented apartment. I was soon out cold as my body told me that my need for sleep trumped any information it was getting about daylight and mealtimes.

When I woke, the hunger issue was buzzing in my brain.

"What do you fancy?" asked Jason. "We can get local food on the corner. Or go down to a restaurant you might like and get a beer as well." That bait won the day.

We headed back down the worn steps, around the corner of the building and out onto Peace Avenue. I was at once struck by the mad traffic, four lanes of it, mostly small cars, many of them taxis, and the crowds on the sidewalks. The unrecognizable language was another element. We weaved our way through the throng, avoiding the many street vendors selling everything from trinkets to lottery tickets, newspapers and magazines.

Apart from the obviously different facial features of the local people, there was little to indicate we were in Asia. Young women were smart and fashionably dressed. The young men wore mostly T-shirts and jeans, with waist-length jackets. Every now and again we saw older men and women clad in shin-length coats with a high collar that ran right around the body and overlapped on the right, fastening at the shoulder.

Jason told me, "It's a *del*, the traditional coat worn by many people, especially older folks." It was strapped at the waist with a leather belt, or in one case a length of bright golden yellow cloth wrapped right round and tucked in tight. Both the men and women who were wearing these outer garments had hats, most of them much like my trilby, and some women sported pretty headscarves. A small, stylized version of the del image appears on all washroom doors in hotels, restaurants and government buildings. Obviously, toilets are unisex in Mongolia.

Jason pointed down and across the street and said, "That's our lunch spot. We'll have to cross through the underpass. It's safer that way."

Right away we skipped down a couple of dozen steps, turned left into the dark tunnel and were at once hit by the smell of urine. Thankfully, we were soon out of that and turned left again, up more steps, to emerge into fresher air. We turned right, went another block east and entered the Chinggis Khan, a poorly lit, cavern-like room that resembled no restaurant I have ever been to.

We were soon seated in deep and encompassing leather armchairs, a low table in front of us. The beer, Chinese Tsingtao, came first. As I scanned the menu I had a few misgivings. One item really caught my eye. It read, "Scream bled eggs." Was this an animal welfare issue? What had been done to the poor chickens? Then it dawned on me as I read down the list and saw a few more aberrations and misspellings of the English language. I could have a plate of scrambled eggs.

CHAPTER 10

Ulaanbaatar City

After that unusual lunch came a must-do call home at the post office. I knew it would be difficult to keep in touch with home once we got into the countryside, because cell phone coverage was not available, so this was important. The line was scratchy, but Jo said all was well in Saskatoon.

Now it was time for more catch-up sleep. The beer helped and I was out cold within seconds of hitting the pillow.

By mid-afternoon I was awake and ready for more exploring. Jason led the way as we took a walk-about in town and did some touristy stuff.

The first stop was a Buddhist temple not far from the apartment. I'd never seen one before. I marvelled at its prayer wheel in the forecourt, the ornate paintwork on the exterior, the monks in their saffron robes, the beautiful artwork inside. It gave a profound feeling of peace. A new and stunning experience.

We hopped into a taxi and five minutes later, heading back the way we came the day before, now towards the airport, came a big surprise. The taxi turned right just before the bridge over the river and stopped outside the fenced garden with a temple-like structure on its far side we'd seen as we entered town. The amazing building, with its many-layered, fluted, faded green roofing with small sculptures along the ridges, was seductive. It looked to me very much like the ornate temples and houses one sees in pictures of Japan and China.

For a trivial 2,000 tugrik (under $1.50 Canadian) we were on our own inside the compound. No guides, no guidebook, nobody else. This was puzzling because almost anywhere else such a building would be a magnet for tourists.

There were missing fence posts around the garden. Inside that the metre-tall stands of grass were turning to brown in the early autumn heat. What a contrast with the old palaces and beautiful stately homes of Europe that I know. Those are seen as a cultural heritage. Their upkeep costs are enormous, so tourists are an important source of revenue. The upkeep costs here in UB must have been almost nil. Considering the importance (to my sense of history anyway) of this place, I was saddened and astonished.

As we got near to the building I saw that the sculptures were animal figurines. The sight of them almost compensated for the unkempt state of the grounds.

There were many extraordinary pictures painted on the eaves around the lowest roof. Beautifully rendered pictures of exotic pheasants, flowers and other figures. A fierce-looking mounted warrior carrying a spear looked over his shoulder at some unseen enemy.

We entered each of the small rooms to admire the objects on display. There were cabinets filled with beautiful decorated ceramics lying next to one another. Old manuscripts sat on shelves. I would have loved to know the history of these objects, but there was no signage on anything, so it was impossible to know their significance or history.

One of the most striking pieces was a statue, no taller than 40 centimetres, of a man in a golden robe, seated on an ornate throne. His red and black scarf flowed down in front. I learned several historical details from Jan Wigsten, who is a dual Mongolian–Swedish citizen. He told me that it was the Choijin Lama Temple Museum and explained the mystery statue. It is of Zanabazar who was first-born of the Bodgo Gegen lineage. His name was converted to Bogd Khan in 1921, when the eighth incarnation became the theocratic leader of independent Mongolia. Zanabazar died in 1924. The communist government of the day decided it should not look for his new incarnation, and the new USSR constitution was adopted. This fitted with Morgan's explanation of the situation of the Tsaatan reindeer herders when the Russians arrived and tried to destroy their ancient culture.

We walked out of the museum, heading towards the post office and Peace Avenue, when I caught sight of an unusual piece of sculpture outside a walled compound. We took our lives in our hands to cross the road, as I wanted to take some photos.

I was well rewarded because the statue, standing alone on its own plinth, was a finely rendered mythical lion as often seen in East Asia. Behind the plinth, set right into the gate of what I learned is called the Children's Garden or Huhtiin Park, the area behind the wall, was a chimera figure of a naked human female mixed with a lion's head and claws. The bushy end of the lion's tail curved up from behind to cover her pubic region. Nobody, not even Jan, has been able to tell me more about the history of this work.

The two very different sculptures are testament to the powerful symbolic nature of the beast in so many aspects of human culture. Considering that the lion's natural range had never been further east than where India's city of Delhi now stands, it's a mystery how lions became so altered over time.

As we stood by the gate, Jason told me about a show that would be performed here a bit later. At six o'clock I could come back to the park and watch a 90-minute show highlighting Mongolian cultural activities. The opportunity was too good to miss, but there was an hour to spare before the program started.

We walked back up Peace Avenue. Halfway to the apartment we reached a pink-painted cafe with the faded name — Chez Bernard — above the window. The name alone was an obvious clue that it catered to Westerners. A light tea and snack was the solution.

After the welcome break, I returned to the Children's Garden, leaving Jason to head to the apartment to sort out things for our flight to the town of Murun (see the map of Mongolia in the photo section) scheduled for 11 o'clock the next day. That would be the real start of my trip into the mountains to work with the reindeer and their herders.

Once through the strange gate, I tagged along with other obvious tourists who seemed to know where they were going (the Mongolian tour guide leading them, flag held above her head, was a clue). I purchased a ticket for the show and thumbed through the brochure. It had some slightly grainy pictures of musicians in gaudy costumes and a young woman in a seemingly impossible body position. I was going to watch the Tumen Ekh ensemble.

We climbed the two flights of stairs to the theatre and I found a spot among the others, all Caucasians, on the middle of three raised sets of steps along one side of the room. The steps were covered in dark blue carpet and looked like up-market bleachers.

The next hour and a half flashed by in an instant. The pictures in the brochure did no justice whatever to the gorgeous multicoloured silks of the performers. There were instruments I'd never seen before making beautiful and haunting sounds I'd never heard before. There were small and large cello and violin-like instruments, each topped by a carving of a horse's head. They had only two strings. There were decorated drums, and wind instruments in a variety of shapes.

There were singers and chanters, and a stunning display of throat singing quite unlike that of the Inuit of Canada, which I have heard both electronically via radio and in person during trips to Baffin Island when working with polar bears. The throat singer was a huge, deep-chested man who produced two different notes at the same time. I have no idea how.

For me, overloaded with new cultural experiences, the most stunning and at the same time disturbing segment of the show was the performance of contortionists. They were girls, two of them perhaps in their early teens, the other older, dressed in diaphanous pale blue or purple costumes that revealed much of their slim bodies, with thicker material over breasts and lower body. A bikini alone would have been less sexy.

The girls began with fairly simple moves to music but soon got into body positions that looked impossible. Their postures became steadily more complex. They started with a leg over the neck, which was no doubt simple for them but looked horribly uncomfortable to me.

Eventually, they were so convoluted, with both legs over their backs, the feet tucked under the folded arms, that I realized the postures they adopted must have taken years of practice and manipulation to achieve. Of course, like trained dancers everywhere they had smiles to light up a room.

Although my right brain was enchanted by their sinuous movements and sheer artistry, my medically bound left brain worried about the long-term effects of the movements and positions of the girls. I could not imagine that their backs would ever be in great shape for carrying heavy loads, or indeed any kind of load.

The most captivating of the dancers was dressed in an astonishing array of coloured silken robes, with a full mask topped by a set of sika deer antlers. As a long-time student of anything to do with deer of any species, this dancer naturally caught my eye. This antler-headed, silken-clad, rainbow-coloured, costumed performer was acting as a shaman. The gyrations and chants lasted for five minutes. Wow!

I returned to the apartment tired and hungry, exhilarated by the show.

"Is there somewhere nearby we can get a bite? I need to head for bed pretty soon, but I need some food first," I asked Jason.

We were soon seated in the Marco Polo restaurant on the ground floor of the apartment block. The table had a cracked plastic cover decorated with red flowers. Cigarette burns on the surface added to the artwork. Pale green melamine plates had similar but irregular adornments. This was not going to be an haute cuisine experience. More like a hole-in-the wall. We waited for the dish of mutton stew that Jason ordered. Some noodles fried in mutton fat accompanied the meat. I knew I was on overload. What I didn't know was that with this dish, called *tsoivan*, I'd planted a time bomb with a slow-burning fuse in my gut.

Next morning we headed for breakfast. Chez Bernard beckoned. Among a Tower of Babel of languages I recognized American-accented English, the guttural sounds of German and the musical lilt of Scandinavian conversation. After a delicious plate of poached eggs, lashings of marmalade on buttered toast and a hot cup of tea, we returned to the apartment to prepare for our onward flight.

We headed back to the airport and boarded an ancient Antonov Russian turbo-prop plane that looked, to my unpractised eye, like that other workhorse of the short ferry, the American DC3. The canvas seats had seen better days; they sagged like an old skirt. My dull gray-greenish safety belt was knotted in the middle and there was no way it could reach its socket.

"We're bound for the town of Murun," Jason explained. "We're flying because Morgan wants us to get on with the work. We could drive, but the roads are not ideal, and the trip would take about 24 hours. The flight takes an hour."

As I later discovered, Jason was being a trifle economic with his comment about the roads.

Murun's airstrip had only a single runway. Another member of our party was waiting to welcome us at the concrete block terminal. She was an attractive, short, dark-haired, young woman named Liliana Goldman. "Call me Lil," she said as we introduced ourselves.

Our driver, solidly built Gala, greeted the two arrivals with a simple "*Sain baina uu*?" which sounded like "Sanbanoo" to my uneducated ear. It is the same as any greeting anywhere in the world. "Hello, how are you?" in English-speaking cultures.

We piled the gear into the back of the small Jeep-like vehicle and turned left out of the airport gate onto a pitted tarmac road. To the right the tarmac ended 25 metres from the gate, and then the road — or more accurately, slightly oversized goat track — disappeared over a grassy crest on the horizon. When I saw this, I wondered what we were in for on our drive north.

As I took an afternoon walk through the town, I began to learn the importance of horses in rural Mongolian life. A single paint horse stood at the entrance to a store with large blue letters in Cyrillic, subtitled "SHOPPING CENTER" in red. Not a vehicle in sight. Then it was back to the apartment building where the team members stay when in Murun, and an early night.

CHAPTER 11

Towards the Taiga

Next morning I woke with a sore belly, nothing critical, just some sort of indigestion. I wasn't sure if my image in the mirror was really green or whether it was a reflection affected by the avocado-coloured wallpaper, much faded over time.

Had I been at home, I would have stayed put, but in this spartan place there was no point in hanging about. And, anyway, Morgan would be worried about us, already a day late, and there was work to do.

By nine o'clock we were on our way. The rear compartment of the little, pale brown, soft-top, Russian Jeep-like vehicle called an UAZ was packed to the gills. Jason and Lil shared the back seat with soft luggage, sleeping bags and coats. Boxes of food, backpacks and my hockey bag full of clothes and veterinary stuff occupied the rear compartment. The sturdy, ancient rattletrap offered no comfort. As if this was not enough, the design engineers must have forgotten about suspension and shock absorbers. My long legs (I'm 182 cm, Lil about 163 and Jason 175) meant I could sit in the front seat, although my knees were jammed against the console for the entire journey. As it turned out this was a mixed blessing. The others had the cushioning of the bags; I could exit in a hurry.

Within five minutes we'd left any signs of town or civilization, going past the airport. The road quickly became a mere gesture. It more or less followed the line of power poles that stretched away over the horizon. We were soon driving across an endless sea of rolling grass-covered hummocks with clumps of low bush dotted here and there, and higher mounds topped by trees.

Half an hour past the airport, what I had thought to be mere indigestion, the fuse ignited by the meal of tsoivan, burned down to the dynamite. The time bomb went off. About every half hour for the next five hours I dove out of the Jeep and headed for the nearest rock, or just simply got behind the vehicle, to deposit DNA on the steppes of central Asia. That front seat exit proved to be vital.

Between the explosive bouts I noted that the vehicle tracks on the scarred landscape looked like a badly braided length of hair. Sometimes six wide, others only two, they wound back and forth, criss-crossing as we and goodness knows how many previous drivers tried to find the best route. We negotiated rocks and the muddy spots where predecessors mired during rain-affected trips.

I thought of how the prairie regions of my home province of Saskatchewan must have looked in the days of the buffalo when the only trees stood beside streams and other bodies of water. Grasslands stretched away to the horizon. This was not a traditional Saskatchewan flatland scene, but more like the rolling hills of the Qu'Appelle Valley or Grasslands National Park through which the Frenchman River flows.

A few times the braids here coalesced into a single track where rocks pushed their way up through the grass and an outcrop or the steep side of a valley made sure that no deviation was advisable.

Every now and again we saw herds of livestock, mainly sheep and goats, sometimes cattle, sometimes all three in one herd. A few skinny dogs wandered around. Each time men on horses rode nearby. Most of the younger ones wore baseball caps, but many had on battered trilby-style hats, made of soft felt with a pinch at the front of the crown. This happens to be not only my favourite style (I have owned a succession of them over the years) but the one I'd brought with me for the trip.

The men looked almost centaur-like on their mounts. The ones on the move sat straight up. Some others, as they watched their precious stock, were more relaxed, almost slouching. When I commented, Lil told me she'd learned that Mongolian horsemen can sit in the saddle for many hours and even sleep there. One of the minders, a teenaged boy sitting with only one bum cheek on the saddle, looked up for a brief moment. I soon realized that, at least in rural Mongolia, if you cannot ride a horse, you are an exception.

Of course, this was the land of the descendants of Chinggis Khan (known in the West as Genghis). His horsemen were so skilled that they could not only shoot arrows while riding forwards but had perfected the extraordinary skill of being able to shoot to kill while retreating, turning back and judging range, arrow arc and the speed of both their own mounts and that of the target.

Later I learned that something over 80 per cent of the almost three million Mongolians have DNA markers of that amazing man. I have tried to calculate the math to show how that figure computes to have left that many descendants after almost 800 years, but it is beyond me.

Ah! The benefits of being an emperor.

Even one of the seven members of my writing group in Saskatoon told me she has a Mongolian ancestor somewhere in her tree. Given the history of the Khan's vast empire, and its spread across the Middle East right up to the gates of Budapest, perhaps her bloodline does trace that far back. She has never had a DNA test done and has no intention of doing so for my sake.

Two oxen harnessed between the poles of wooden carts appeared beside us. I soon realized that the never-ending bumping was going to give my lower back and kidney area a very thorough workout, while my neck was in danger of imminent whiplash. If it wasn't rocks, it was the randomly repeated lurches from side to side as we switched tracks, or one or more wheels caught in some slightly deeper rut.

Between the vital and rapid departures from the front seat, I closed my eyes and imagined the reputed benefits of having a masseuse, maybe a beautiful young woman, walk up and down my spine. The image disappeared as we pitched again.

We had not seen another vehicle for six hours. I knew almost nothing of what lay in front of me and cared less. I just wanted to get on with the journey, get to work and knew (assumed) that the internal earthquakes would eventually settle down. Little did I know that there is but one community between Murun and our destination of Tsagaan Nuur, so when we rolled into Ulaan-Uul in the late afternoon, much delayed by my numerous excursions, I was in no condition to complain or notice anything. Dehydration and a total mess-up in my body's electrolyte balance had reduced me to a barely conscious mumbling lump of flesh. The whole-body massage I'd been through did not help.

Luckily, Lil had been this way before and had a friend in the village, so we diverted to their house, where Lil was greeted like a long-lost daughter, Jason welcomed and Gala acknowledged as a fellow countryman. I was gently led to a bed and wrapped in my sleeping bag. While the rest of the party visited and enjoyed each other's company, I lay in a semi-coma, waking every now and again to take a sip of water. I felt as if I had been reamed out with a stiff wire brush from tonsils to tailbone. At least the bed wasn't moving, a great relief.

By morning my condition improved enough that I could accept my first cup of tea and a small crumb of dry bread. Still feeling weak but realizing that we couldn't delay any longer, I gingerly climbed into the front seat for more rock and roll. Every few kilometres trees appeared in the landscape. Most were larch, close relatives to the tamarack of North America, still mainly green in late August but showing signs of their upcoming turn to golden yellow, with the odd pine among them. The pines, as we continued north, appeared more frequently. Along the banks of a couple of watercourses and on the shores of the lakes we passed there were some willows and a species of poplar not unlike the ones back home in Canada.

The road headed towards a bigger stand of trees, almost all larch, but before we entered we stopped beside a four-metre high, pyramid-shaped stack of logs and dead wood that looked almost as if someone had prepared a bonfire. It was obviously not intended for that purpose because it was festooned with numerous lengths of the same blue cloth I saw wrapped around the rear-view mirror in the taxis in UB, as well as the sun visor in the UAZ.

"What's that?" I asked. Lil explained, "It's an *ovoo*, a religious shrine. Devout Buddhist travellers are expected to walk round it three times in a clockwise direction."

Indeed, Gala stopped and did just that, offering no word of explanation. Lil and Jason followed, out of respect, but I left them to it. I knew I should also take the walk, but I was still a sort of wet bundle of spaghetti and not feeling strong enough.

Not 50 metres from the ovoo, we headed up a steep rocky track among the larch, and the road split into two lanes around a tree. Over the crest it descended in a steepish incline near the border between the trees and the grasslands and I caught sight of a pair of huge brown steppe eagles, the white bar across each wing making identity certain. While one sat on a dead branch not 30 metres from us, a second bird soared above. It was my first sighting of this huge bird, very reminiscent of the tawny eagle of Africa that I know much better. Majestic.

I was beginning to get used to the wide open spaces as I compared the scene to the four lanes of nonstop traffic during rush hour in any major Western city. I'd not seen a soul, not even a herder, for a couple of hours, perhaps because I'd nodded off, maybe a few times, when I was jerked awake and looked to my right as the Jeep came to a halt.

A blue motorcycle and sidecar sat just off the track to our right. A slim man clad in a gray del, topped by a battered trilby, walked over from the bike. The standard "Sain baina uu?" greeting was followed by a rapid discussion and gestures towards the bike beside which a middle-aged woman, presumably his wife, dressed in a dark purple del, sat quietly on the grass. Gala opened up the back of the Jeep, pulled out the assorted luggage and scrabbled in the well under the floor. He soon stood with a triumphant look on his face and a small bolt in his hand. The two men walked back to the bike and bent over the engine for little more than a minute. They stood as one and a moment later, after the stranger made a couple of thrusts on the kick-starter, the engine fired, coughed twice and settled into a steady roar, breaking the utter silence of that almost empty landscape.

With a quick nod and an unheard word or two, Gala turned back and the couple vanished from view over yet another rounded hill to who knows where.

We continued on our way north.

More hours went by as we bumped and ground our way across the "road." Our next unscheduled stop, at about two o'clock, occurred right on a crudely made bridge over a small stream. Whoever laid the logs wasn't thinking about wheeled transport. They lay straight along the direction of our drive, not across it. They were also not fixed or nailed in any way. Before we reached the apex of the pile, the right-hand wheels slipped between two logs. We were hung up, going nowhere. With Jason lending a hand, the use of one of the logs as a lever and Lil and I staying well clear, Gala, a big, powerful man, had us out of that little mess in no time at all.

Away to our right a long line of snow-capped mountains jutted above the grasslands like a row of shark's teeth, and silver-coloured lakes began to appear. I turned my head to talk to Lil and asked about them.

"Those are the Hovsgol Mountains that lie to the south and west of the lake of the same name," she said. "The lake, Mongolia's largest, is claimed by some to be deeper than even Baikal in Russia, which lies only about 200 kilometres northeast. It used to carry small freighters on commercial shipping runs."

As we bounced along, I asked Lil to tell me more about her musical connection to the country. "I'm a jazz flutist," she said. "I came here to work with an ancient art form called the Long Song, in Mongolian, *Urtiin duu*. It's an integral part of Mongolian musical tradition, important in many situations. It's played on the two-string or horse-head fiddle that you saw in UB. I met with a gentleman named Dad'suren at the School for Traditional Music that bears his name. His specialty is to play tunes that will persuade an animal that has not accepted her newborn to lick it dry and let down her milk for it to get that first crucial drink."

I was hypnotized by this unusual, fascinating account. As Lil let me interject and ask questions, I tried to process the idea of a flute being used as jazz instrument. Then I remembered my favourite radio program, *As It Happens*, which airs on CBC each weekday evening. Its theme music is a jazz flute piece called "Curried Soul" by Moe Koffman. I could hear it in my mind's ear as we rode.

More lakes, more tree stands, a yak-pulled cart loaded with a bed and other household goods, one minivan-type vehicle going back towards Ulaan-Uul and a lot more grasslands. Later we started to see fenced-off hayfields, and cattle, yaks and one of their huge hybrids grazing together.

"That's a khainag," said Lil. "They're a cross between a yak and a cow. They're bigger and hardier than either parent. They produce more milk that is lower in fat than a yak's."

We crossed another bridge, skirted another water body and drove into Tsagaan Nuur in time for supper. It stood right beside a crystal-clear lake called Dood Tsagaan. All of the buildings were wooden, some log cabins, most of boards with roofing paper and tiles or wooden shingles. The only two-story one was the school, located in the middle of the village. "There's a very high literacy rate, even here among the rural folks," explained Lil. The roads were no better organized here than out on the steppe, and there was plenty of evidence of previous wet conditions.

The importance of horses again came home to me as we crossed the centre of the village. Several were tethered to poles and rails, and three mounted men crossed in front of us, all going in different directions as we slowly negotiated the ruts. The odour of horse manure wafted through the window of the Jeep. It isn't something that bothers me (how could it in my profession?) and once more emphasized the role of horses in rural Mongolia. I didn't ask the others how they felt about it.

We pulled up at the building that would be our quarters for the night. The inn, as the Americans called it, bore no resemblance to ones I have imagined or any I have seen elsewhere. There was no painted sign, and the roof was badly in need of repair, unless the gaps in the roofing tiles and the torn black paper were intended to provide a form of air conditioning. Luckily, I never had to witness its waterproof qualities. Inside there were two rather cramped rooms, one of which served as a dormitory, with narrow wooden slat beds along the walls.

Parked outside stood a khaki-coloured Forgan van, another leftover from the days of Russian dominance. It would also be our transport for the next leg of the trip.

A relieved Morgan came out to greet us. "We were worried about you," she said. "What happened?" I realized that this far out in the countryside there was no cell phone communication.

We were introduced to the innkeeper, Nyamaa, an attractive woman in her mid-40s. We met another party member, our translator Binde, a young woman wearing a smart red jacket and jeans, of about the same age as the three Americans. As both Morgan and Lil spoke what sounded to me like fluent Mongolian, I wondered about her role. I later learned that Binde did indeed have an important part to play, as the two American women had not quite mastered a difficult tongue and, like me, Jason was making his first trip to the country.

After the normal greetings, my next priority was a wash. I must have smelt like the leavings of last week's wolf kill, so I stripped off and tried to clean up with a body wash, using my own soap and face cloth as best I could, standing beside an enamel bowl of cold water. While I was in my all-together, Lil came in from the dining area, took a horrified look, uttered a loud squawk and hastily departed.

As my sleeping bag beckoned, I crashed onto the nearest unclaimed bed, just boards 30 centimetres off the floor, set on four legs, after stuffing my luggage underneath it. A couple of hours later, I managed some more dry bread. No more mutton-fried noodles for this boy. Ever.

I also had some work to do to prepare for our trip into the mountains. The big bag full of stuff had to be sorted. It was way over the usual size-limited luggage allowance, but maybe the hockey-mad Canadians in Saskatoon had thought I was going on a coaching trip and simply ignored the airline rules.

Full of syringes, needles and surgical instruments, I'm not quite sure how it passed through security, but here it was. My journey from Saskatoon started only a couple weeks shy of the three-year anniversary of the horrors of the destruction of New York's Twin Towers and the attack on the Pentagon, generally known as 9/11. Perhaps it passed because all my bits and pieces were in boxes.

Morgan showed me a map of the area around Tsagaan Nuur (see the map of Mongolia that shows the detail in the photo section). She had already explained that we would spend up to ten days in one region of the mountains and return to the inn to revamp before heading into the other. She pointed out the regions, divided by the Shished River, that are locally known as the *Barone* (west) and *Zuun* (east) taiga. They are both in the Sayan Mountains that straddle the border between Mongolia and Russia. At times we would be less than ten kilometres from Russia.

The border had been so tightly controlled that no one had deliberately crossed it in almost 70 years. Morgan's story about the hunters who mistakenly wandered into Russian territory and spent a month in jail made me hope that we wouldn't make the same mistake.

Having read both plenty of John le Carré and Aleksandr Solzhenitsyn's *The Gulag Archipelago*, I at once imagined being chucked into a Russian prison in Siberia and more or less being left to rot while freezing my buns in winter and being eaten alive by mosquitos and blackflies in summer.

Morgan also told us that when the border restrictions were somewhat lowered she witnessed an emotional meeting between a brother and sister who had been separated by that border for almost 70 years, while living only 20 kilometres apart.

At about four o'clock, after some more dry bread, and a daring slurp of peanut butter, as well as a post-prandial nap, I headed out to the lake, only a couple of hundred metres from the inn. I wasn't just going to see the beautiful view of the far-off mountains but was armed with two sets of fishing gear, a four-weight fly rod, a box of flies and a lightweight spinning outfit. Note: I virtually never travel anywhere without fishing poles, and after a few years of searching have finally found multi-section rods that can easily be carried, even in a briefcase.

I tried a couple of wet flies, even a grasshopper imitation, but none of the lake residents showed any interest. Being very much a catch and eat, not a catch and release, fisherman, after a fruitless hour, I switch to a red and white spoon and soon had a nice string of half-kilo silvery spotted trout-like specimens on the shore. Two small boys joined me, but all we could do was smile and gesture. The boys said something that sounded like "lenok" to me, and Binde confirmed that this is the correct name.

I took the catch back to the inn and showed them to Nyamaa, who knew what's what without the help of translation. There were two more fish than we needed for our working group and with hand gestures I indicated that she should share them with her family. An hour later she appeared with our supper. A welcome surprise for all. It was also the last meal of any fresh protein (other than reindeer milk) that we ate for the next ten days, until we spent another night at the inn.

Once more I crashed, exhausted but more or less recovered from three exhausting days of travel to get to our jump-off point where the reindeer work would begin.

In the morning we headed down the river on the next leg of our journey.

CHAPTER 12
Riders First

Thankfully, after a restful night, the time bomb had completely fizzled out. We five passengers were packed and ready to roll on the next leg of the trip. As we knew we would return before heading to the west taiga, I left half my veterinary supplies under the bunk. Gala organized the luggage in the back of the Forgan. There were sleeping bags, backpacks crammed with clothing, food, and coats of various hues and sizes. We could never have all fitted into the little "Jeep," even without the gear. By the time were all aboard there was no room to move.

We stopped at a little log cabin store. Inside was a single counter behind which stood a middle-aged woman wearing a gray del and a bright scarf with red and yellow stripes. On the shelf behind her and along the adjacent wall stood a limited selection of nonperishable household items: cigarettes, some foodstuffs in tins and plastic packages.

Morgan picked up many packets of ramen noodles for the group. I chose half a dozen bars of chocolate for comfort food. There were no brands I recognized, but brightly coloured packets of Golden Gobi milk chocolate caught my eye. The striking artwork on the red and gold wrapper had three Bactrian camels, the two-humped variety common to the central steppes of Asia, standing staring at some distant spot, maybe the horizon. Still unfamiliar tugriks changed hands as I stuffed the bars into my day pack.

"We have to cross the Shished River that flows west out of the lake and then drive away to our base to pick up our horses," Morgan explained. "Bayanmunk, our horse guide [the local term for a wrangler], will be there with his string."

Because of my lack of experience with riding, I was already slightly nervous about the notion of spending the next three weeks in the saddle, but there was no other way to make the trip.

When we met in Saskatoon back in the summer, Morgan told me about Nansalmaa, a Mongolian vet employed by a government department based in UB. She had been working with the Tsaatan on their reindeer problems for a few years. "She will be with us on this trip into the mountains and will meet us in Tsagaan Nuur." I soon found out we had some rather different approaches to the deers' medical problems.

It was therefore no surprise when we stopped at another log house and picked her up. I guessed her to be in her early 50s. She wore a well-used, dark cerise del. Very much a working garment, slightly ragged at the edges and held around her middle by an old leather belt. Her headscarf had a red and green pattern on a white background. No trace of gray hair, but the wind-gouged lines in her face showed her years of field experience. We were now a party of seven. I thought the van was already full, but of course not. The attitude here was nothing compared to vehicle packing in Africa. In Kenya I have seen 16 people carried in and on a short-wheel-based Land Rover designed for six. In back some passengers were stacked three deep. The heads of the top layer touched the roof. They sat on the laps of the middle lot, who were perched on those sitting on the actual seats. In front three passengers and the driver had relative comfort. How the driver managed the gear stick remains a mystery to this day. Never mind the humans, on the roof rack there were several bags of charcoal, chickens tied by the legs and two goats.

After a 20-minute drive along the shore and riverbank we arrived at the place where the lake rushes out and turns into a river. The ferry was unusual, like none I've ever seen. Thick planks lay lengthways on a metal frame. They were attached to two huge drums that looked like bowser tanks cannibalized from fuel trucks. The drums were the flotation devices. One of the ferrymen held a three-centimetre braided cable running through a pulley wheel. On each bank the cable was anchored to cement blocks set into the ground.

The whole thing looked as if the eccentric cartoonist William Heath Robinson had designed it, but it worked because we could see it heading our way. There were three horses, the riders still up, on board.

We passengers climbed out of the van while Gala edged his way up the boarding ramp and stopped in the middle of the planks. A mother and her two little girls joined us, and we all walked up the ramp. The oldest girl, dressed in a gorgeous bright blue del, her pigtails hanging out and down like bloodhound's ears, looked across the river as we set off.

The ferrymen soon got to work by grabbing the cable and pulling hand over hand to move us across the 60 or so metres of fast-flowing water. Within another half-hour we reached the end of the now nonexistent road. By this time I recognized the deep truth of wolverine researcher Rebecca Watters's comment about the properties of the Forgan. In one of her blogs she wrote about sitting in "Russian vans — the world's most uncomfortable motorized contraptions." I guess she'd never had the pleasure of riding in a Jeep-like UAZ.

The track dipped down and we forded a small stream, about a metre wide. We soon entered a plot of land surrounded by a simple post and two-rail fence. We were at a permanent home, not a camp.

The home in the foreground and the gradual slope behind with a big stand of larch to the right made a striking sight. Less than a kilometre away to our north the hills stretched away to the horizon. The delicate green spikes of the trees were halfway turned to the golden-yellow of their autumn and early winter coats.

The main building was the *ger*, a large, round, tent-like structure made of heavy canvas. It was white, like the others we'd seen along the way, some four metres tall at the peak of the sloping roof. A metal chimney poked up just off centre. There were two outbuildings constructed of pine planks. Several extra planks lay on the ground nearby. On a metal pole near the ger wind turbine blades slowly spun, driven by a zephyr.

Several horses, tethered to a rail fence surrounding a corral, stood saddled up ready to go. Close up they looked no larger than the Welsh pony I rode as a boy of 9 in Germany, where my military father was stationed at the time. They were more solidly built than Max, that boyhood mount, but no taller.

Three men clad in dels stood nearby. Morgan introduced me, but the rapidly spoken names were difficult to catch. The only words I understood were "Doctor Haigh." We exchanged handshakes and "Sain baina uu," which I had now mastered. I soon learned their names. Bayanmunk the wrangler stood next to his horses. His well-worn bucket hat tilted back. A dark green del was tied around his waist with a green *boos* (belt).

A second, slower, introduction helped me get the names of the other two men. Ganbat and Borkhuu. Ganbat with high cheekbones and a long narrow face. Borkhuu, the shorter of the two with a rounder face. He had a cigarette on the go. Both wore hats similar to my own battered green trilby. Borkhuu's tilted to the left. Morgan explained, "They are veterinary technicians. Borkhuu is from here, the east taiga region. He will also travel with us into the west. I hope you can help them with some teaching and techniques. They took a two-month tech course in the capital a few years back." Together with Gala, the three of them emptied the van and took the gear over beside the horses.

Behind me I heard little voices. Two girls, the bigger probably no more than 8 years old, headed up from the stream, clambered through the fence, picked up a milk churn of water and carried it between them, each leaning out at an angle to distribute the weight. The taller one braced her arm against the shoulder of the younger one.

They headed to the ger. Its heavy canvas outer layer was tied around with three lines of rope and held by a few guy lines that didn't seem to add much to the overall strength, although I suspected they might come into play when the wind blew hard. The pole supporting the wind turbine had an electric line snaking down and across to disappear under the bottom of the tent.

The door, made of beautifully decorated wood, had intricate blue and white whorls in vertical rows painted on a bright red background. I stooped to enter because it was only 1.2 metres high and wide enough to admit only one person at a time.

If the door was finely crafted, the interior was a real eye-opener. Behind all the furniture a seemingly continuous circle of a thin wooden trellis provided some rigidity to the canvas wall. It looked very much like the sort of thing we use at home to support climbing plants growing on the south side of our house. A two-centimetre-thick layer of felt ran all the way round between the trellis and the canvas. The roof was supported by a series of slats that radiated out and down from the top of a centre pole to join the tops of the trellis. A metal wood-burning stove sat to the right of the pole, its chimney disappearing through the roof. Three metal-framed single beds with thin mattresses stood back to back along the left wall. They looked exactly like the ones I slept in as a schoolboy.

Opposite the door was a small altar with a bright gold statue of the Buddha and some of that same blue cloth that seemed to be everywhere in Mongolia. My eye continued its clockwise scan. There were some brightly decorated chests with drawers, a mirror on top of one. A 50-centimetre, black and white television on another. Beneath this one, battery cables snaked towards and under the side where the turbine was located.

Then a couple more beds and, finally, back near the door, a kitchen and cooking area where pots and pans, toiletries — toothpaste the most obvious — and utensils in cloth hangers were tied to the trellis. Split logs were stacked beside the door, and small, brightly coloured carpets and framed photos hung all around the home. Stunning and unexpected.

A woman whose name I never learned pointed to one of the beds, inviting me to sit.

On top of the stove a large metal dish that looked similar to the cooking bowls I know well from my Kenya days was bubbling away. Like a giant wok it had a rounded contour, without a flat bottom, and fitted neatly into the opening on top of the stove. In Kiswahili, it's called a *karai* and serves the same purpose as it does in Mongolia. Our hostess lifted a shiny block of something black from the area behind her. About 20 by 30 centimetres, no more than five centimetres thick, it resembled a rich fruitcake or a big chunk of packed dates. She cut off a thin slice with a sharp knife, dropped it into a mortar and ground briefly with the pestle then dropped the flakes into the water. Binde explained, "That's tea." A few minutes later, our hostess poured some milk from a small churn, stirred the mixture and ladled the brew from the stovetop into little china bowls. She carried the bowls, one at a time, to each of us.

Morgan (who gave me lots of tips on proper cultural behaviour as we went along) had warned me to accept any offering. "If the object is heavy, you can either grasp it in both hands or grip your right wrist with your left hand for support. To accept with the left hand would be a no-no."

Some of the other behaviours I had to adopt right away were essential. Morgan also warned me to enter a ger or any other dwelling during our trip to the left, because the right-hand side is reserved for the family and especially for the hostess. I must never, she stressed *never*, do anything with the fire. That's the hostess's territory.

There were other things. It's impolite to point your feet at anyone, or especially the fire, so you must sit with them tucked under yourself. Your hat must be placed with the brim down because if it faces up the good luck will pour out.

She further explained that in some homes the tea could be laced with salt. "You must take a sip," she said. "If you don't like it, simply put it down beside you and ignore it. No one will be offended as long as you take that sip." I took the bowl with my right hand. Happily, there was no added salt.

As we drank our tea, Lil took the conversation in a slightly different direction with her account of a similar cultural requirement when offered *airag*, fermented mare's milk. I'll leave the results of her tale of overindulgence in this potent brew to the imagination, but it wasn't pretty. I was very glad to have had the warning, when, on my own little trip into the edge of the Gobi two years later, I was able to take a very small sip and then put the bowl aside. I noticed that my translator on that trip, a young woman named Ankha, did exactly the same, while our driver Ulzii obviously had a taste for it.

With tea all done, we left the ger and walked to the fenced area by the horses. Borkhuu stubbed out his roll-your-own underfoot and moved to join the men, who were tying the gear firmly to the packsaddles of half a dozen horses with several lengths of rope. My bag, stretching from shoulder to hip on a dark bay, took up one side.

As for our own saddles, I'd never seen one like those on the riding horses. I was used enough to the high pommel Western saddles of North America, and Max's saddle had been the traditional English kind. Here there were two distinct styles. The most striking, a traditional Mongolian one with intricately decorated wooden pieces that reached up a good 15 centimetres fore and aft. The others had metal arches in front of and behind the leather seat. "That's one of the old Russian military type," explained Morgan.

The latter was past its sell-by date and to the bum-breaking surface a cushion had been added. This would prove to be important. The saddle, with a blanket under it, was tied to the horse with a variety of lengths of rawhide rope cinched down, and a single twisted strap tightened with a buckle. I suppose I'd have called the mishmash a girth. The reins were unusual. Made up of knotted lengths of gray rawhide that to my inexperienced eyes looked very short.

Morgan described another cultural norm. "You must never step over a horse's reins. It's simply taboo." She then asked Bayanmunk a brief question in Mongolian as she turned towards me, pointing to a bay gelding standing quietly with the group.

"That's your horse," she said, "and don't ever call him a pony."

"Has he got a name?" I asked to no one in particular.

Binde replied at once. "No horse ever gets named in Mongolia."

"Why?"

"There are just too many of them."

This was the moment. I had been worrying about this phase of the trip for quite some time. It would be fair to say that I'm an inexperienced rider. Apart from a single one-hour session on one of my neighbour's horses a week before leaving home I had not ridden a horse for 53 years. A half-day outing in 1950 near Hanover with Max was my first proper session in the saddle. Here I was faced with several multi-hour days on a seat and mount that weren't quite what I'd anticipated.

I looked at Morgan. "I'm a bit worried. Please ask Bayanmunk to keep an eye on me. I haven't ridden horse since I was 9 years old."

"Don't worry," she said as she turned back to the man who would have my welfare in his hands for the next three weeks. In rapid and what sounded like seamless Mongolian she spoke a few sentences.

He gave a wide-eyed grin, nodded and offered me a leg up as I mounted.

We set off, up the hill, close to the edge of the larch forest. Pretty soon the group strung out, but Bayanmunk held back, not far behind me, no doubt playing mother hen, as much for his horse as for me. After all I was, by their standards, a big guy, at least ten kilos heavier than anyone else in the party. The saddle was more comfortable than I expected, but the metal loop on the Russian saddle worried me a bit, being very close to my belly. However, it soon proved useful, as the metal arch gave me something to grab when we rode up or down the many steep slopes that were part of our route over the next while. My anxiety level soon diminished, as muscle memory and the actual feel of the horse became second nature.

As we crested the first rise, Binde dropped back to chat. "You know," she said, "Morgan got her numbers mixed up when she translated your request. What she actually said was 'This man feels like he is 9 again when he gets on a horse.'"

I guess translating numbers into Mongolian is a bit tricky.

CHAPTER 13

Into the Mountains

The challenge of riding turned out not to be as hard as I'd feared. The expected brutal attack on my nether regions by the saddle was minimal. I would not be singing falsetto by the time I reached home.

Within a day I was comfortable and content, although still grabbing the metal arches in the front of the saddle on a steep uphill, or if the group decided, just for the hell of it, to break into a canter. My mount was obviously used to carrying heavy loads over endless distances.

Before I left on this new adventure, my neighbour at home, an experienced horseman, tipped me off about avoiding the chafing on my inner thighs by telling me to wear long johns. The polypropylene ones I'd used for years during the depths of the Saskatchewan winter proved ideal.

We climbed over grasslands and up through tree stands before emerging onto yet more open country. Snow-capped mountains appeared in the distance.

Then a surprise, something I'd not thought about for years. A bog, a high-altitude bog. The last one I'd encountered was on the slopes of Mount Kenya, at an elevation of some 3000 metres, starting right above the treeline. In under 50 metres during that climb we went from the firm footing of the mixed hardwood tropical forest to open grassland with tussocks. My climbing companions warned me that this part of the climb was called the vertical bog, and at first I wondered about this name. Then I stepped off a tussock and sank to mid-thigh in black ooze. The name is spot on.

My thoughts quickly came back to the present as my horse began to struggle in the mire. Within a very few metres he was muck from his feet to his hocks. If at this point his saddle had not started to slip sideways all might have been okay. I knew this was bad news and luckily, or not, my rugby instincts kicked in. After 25 years of playing the game (although not for many years), I kicked out of my stirrups and threw myself off to one side. It would not have garnered ten, or even one, style points in an Olympic diving competition, but it worked, sort of. My face plant in the black mud was at least soft, if mucky.

The horse, no doubt relieved to be rid of my 94 kilos, carried on a short way. He was dealing with a second problem. The saddle continued its journey round his midriff. This obviously upset him as his feet tangled in the bits and pieces. He turned, heading for the drier ground he'd just left. Inevitably, the turn went through a full 180 degrees and I could now imagine being trampled. Again, those rugby muscle memories saved me. I rolled away as if I was in the bottom of a scrum. Now I was filth all down my back, but the horse missed me and soon found the little brush-covered ridge we'd crossed before hitting the bog.

Bayanmunk, Borkhuu and Ganbat quickly had him in hand, the saddle off, replaced in the correct spot and properly tightened. As Morgan said something to the men in her fluent Mongolian, I cleaned up my face as best I could and half-waded, half-clambered on the tussocks where everyone else was waiting.

My waterproof gaiters kept my trouser legs and socks more or less dry. There were murmurs of sympathy from the Americans and the question, "Are you okay?" Bayanmunk looked concerned. I'm not sure if he felt a trifle embarrassed about the less-than-tight saddle girth. Borkhuu and Ganbat were probably too polite to say anything. They even managed to keep straight faces. We were soon on our way.

Again Binde sidled up and gave me an accurate translation of Morgan's words to the men: "You must look after this doctor. He has come all the way from Canada to help with sick reindeer and he is 103 years old."

Numbers again.

After the drama with the saddle in the swamp, we rode for half an hour on a well-used path that meandered along a slope heading down to a small stream. We came to a camp where a white conical tent, some four metres tall, stood on a flat piece of ground about 20 metres below a log cabin. I was surprised and intrigued by the structure. Its supporting wooden poles emerged in a tight bunch at the peak. It looked almost exactly like the tipis I'm used to seeing at First Nations festivals in Canada. Binde told me it was an *urts*.

There are some differences. The most obvious, from a distance, was the lack of smoke flaps. In North America tipi doors are usually oval in shape. An adult would have to bend low to enter. Here the door was between two of the support poles, part of the main structure. Wider at the base, going up in a triangle, stitched across at head height. A horizontal length of wood held a canvas flap that could be drawn across, thus closing the tent.

I thought we were going to work with reindeer, so the sight of five somewhat scrawny dairy cows tethered nearby was a surprise. Not a reindeer anywhere.

The inside of the dwelling was laid out in much the same way as the ger. Hanging on a rope tied across at head height between poles were stitched holders, one with toothpaste and brushes, another with kitchen utensils. The top section of an antler had been drafted for use as hooks for a milk churn and a red and silver thermos flask.

Our hostess, Aruna, prepared a dish of tea. She mixed something in a bowl and flopped several spoonfuls, one at a time, onto a flat pan. Soon everyone was enjoying delicious fried pancake-like bread that at once reminded me of chapatis and harkened back to many a good curry.

Before long, after some discussion among the locals, I was asked to look at the cows, specially their udders. Aruna said she had not been able to milk two of them for several days. I knelt to examine them. Just about everyone else joined in from the other side. It was at once obvious why I'd been asked.

The teats did not look right. Each hind one had ugly dark red sores that looked like clotted blood. On top of that there were numerous rough little nodules all over their surfaces. No wonder the cow didn't want anyone to touch them. I'd never seen such things on an udder before, but the picture of cowpox in one of my university textbooks from 40 years back promptly appeared in front of me.

The mystery deepened until I asked Aruna, via Binde, if she'd had similar sores on her hands. When she nodded her head up and down, a link connected in my brain. I knew that small rodents, particularly marmots, were a popular dietary item here. I also knew that they are often infected with a virus condition known as cowpox, which can occur in humans and is often acquired by them when they handle a rodent.

Another flap opened in my mind's door, reminding me of the brilliant insight of the English physician Edward Jenner at the end of the 18th century. He is credited with saving the lives of more people than anyone else, ever. His vaccination of people with cowpox material proved effective in preventing smallpox in humans. He tested his idea when he realized that milkmaids did not succumb to the deadly scourge that killed so many people and left any survivors with horrific scars. The milkmaids were probably infected with the cowpox virus and thus immune from the deadlier disease. The two viruses are closely related.

All I needed to do was snip small pieces of a few scabs and drop them into formalin containers that would preserve them until they reach a lab. There was a problem. I had not packed any formalin in Saskatoon. Not good.

Getting samples to send to a lab could be simple, so I decided to take some anyway, in the hope that we could somehow keep them cold in stream or snow as we travelled.

I was wrong about the simple. These cows must have been used to the large horseflies that lived around here. When one of these pests drives his mouthparts into the skin, it feels like a sharp nail being driven into one's hide. The cows knew all about this and developed effective strategies. Not only do they swish their tails as do all cattle bothered by flies but they kick. Hard. Moreover, a cow can kick forwards as effectively as it can backwards.

The flying hoof just missed my head.

Now it was time for action if I was to get the samples. I demonstrated to Borkhuu and Ganbat and we soon had tied the ropes that held the baggage together until we had about five metres. I draped them over the cow's neck and ran them between her legs, then over her back in a criss-cross loop. From there the rope went down and out between her hind legs. Bayanmunk obviously wanted to participate. I asked with signs and he quickly made a temporary rope halter. We held it as the two vet techs pulled backwards. I kept a close eye on her head, ready to help control it as she dropped to the ground, which she soon did. Bayanmunk instantly moved to hobble her hind legs and, as she lay on her side, I collected the samples.

I had not anticipated the reaction. The procedure is one I have carried out dozens of times since it was first demonstrated during my first year of veterinary school in 1959. None of the Mongolians had seen it before. *Oohs!* and *Aahs!* and obviously enthusiastic comments in Mongolian were followed by eager repetition of the technique as we moved to the next animal for collection of more samples.

With this action I'd made a first step of Morgan's request to give advice to the two technicians.

I stood to stretch my back after all the kneeling and crouching.

Meanwhile, Nansalmaa opened her bag, took a few crystals of potassium permanganate from a small container and dropped them into a bowl of water. She then used a big syringe to suck up the pale purple fluid and sprayed the udders of the patients. The fluid is often used for skin conditions and has an antiseptic effect. She then took out a small jar containing white zinc oxide paste and smeared some over the udder. The paste would help to allay any itching and also provide some antibacterial effects. Both can speed healing, but even without any treatment, the scabs would soon disappear and the teats, apart from some thickening, would look normal. The important thing was Aruna knowing that something was being done to help.

After the break I pulled a few pipe cleaners I'd picked up at the dollar store in Saskatoon from the small backpack containing my simple personal stuff. Aruna's children, 12-year-old Otis and her young brothers, sat captivated near the door of the urts as I twisted the multi-coloured pieces into the rough shape of a reindeer, antlers and all.

After all the exertion, we headed into the urts. Morgan poured boiling water over four packets of ramen noodles. Once in my bowl, they had the look and consistency of strips of thin cardboard run through a shredder and then dunked in water. Careful turning over of the strands revealed a few small chunks of some sort of red stuff that looked like broken bits of a child's plastic toy. As for taste, what taste? In comparison, for me, straight tofu would be a gourmet meal in any kind of taste test. Michelin three-star for sure.

Aruna fried up a bunch more of her delicious chapatis. Thank goodness for something to assure me that my taste buds were still functioning.

It was soon bedtime for me. The family headed up to the log cabin and Aruna invited us to use the urts. Our bags emerged from their stuff sacks. The thermal mattresses were pumped up. I have no idea how long the others continued to chat. It'd been quite a day. I was soon out cold.

CHAPTER 14

First Reindeer

As I rubbed the sleepy dust out of my eyes, I saw Aruna working by the stove. She dropped two more split logs into its belly and put on the big metal bowl. Water followed. She soon gave us tea and then produced a nut-brown loaf of bread. It looked like a giant bagel and had a tangy, delicious flavour. A great way to start the day.

We headed out after the horses had been loaded and saddled. Within half a kilometre we reached the bed of a small stream and rode across, straight up the far bank into the trees. Less than 100 metres later we stopped where a spring squirted clear water out of the hillside. A few strips of blue cloth were draped over bushes right above it.

The Mongolians dismounted. Binde and Bayanmunk walked over to the edge of the shallow stream and bent over to drink directly from the rock-strewn water. Morgan explained that one must take a drink from such a sacred spot without using one's hands as a cup.

Ten metres to our left another gush of water jetted out. Across the face of this spring, just below where the water flowed out among the earth between gray rocks, rough-cut boards were jammed between large boulders across the face of the slope. They formed an effective sluice through which the crystal-clear water tumbled from small waterfalls. The water cascaded over a couple of steps before it entered a hollowed-out half log that acted as a pipe. Nansalmaa leant over to drink, again not using her hands.

We were soon on our way up the slope between the trees. In less than 15 minutes I watched as those ahead of me again dismounted.

This time we were beside an ovoo almost four metres tall. Dozens of logs of various length and diameters leant against each other in the shape of a pyramid. Blue cloths were festooned all over the structure. There were many flat boards hung all around it on bits of rope. I walked up to take a closer look.

On every one of them somebody had taken time and trouble to carve an image. Among these was a tiger, a wapiti, two swans stretched out in flight, even a dragon. There weren't only animals. All had writing and other features. Mountains, flowers, whorls and squiggles.

This was obviously an important religious shrine. But it was a surprise because I had learned that the Tsaatan practise shaman- ism, not Buddhism. Yet the blue is known as a Buddhist blessing.

We all circled the ovoo three times. The smokers lit up. The tethered horses nibbled on the trees or reached down to grab a bite of grass.

Four hours and three valleys later, thankfully with no more bogs, we rounded a ridge and saw two urts standing on flat ground. There were a few pine trees in the background.

I'd seen domesticated reindeer in Finland and at home in Saskatchewan, but what I learned in the next month was quite new.

A group of reindeer, the first I'd seen on this trip, was grazing nearby. Our horses, tied to rails, relieved of their loads, shook themselves and stood quietly. Jason sorted the gear. Borkhuu lit up again and we entered the urts.

After a bowl of tea and a lengthy conversation, all in Mongolian, Morgan shifted to English and asked if I was ready to get started. Now was the time to take out the brucella test kits.

From what I'd been able to find out, this nasty disease is a problem here. Morgan's story of the woman who had to leave the taiga and other accounts made it almost certain. After the emails and friendly conversations with my colleague Dr. Bob Dietrich in Alaska, it was just a question of using the cards. The field conditions were not great. It was nowhere near the 21ºC temperature he advised as being essential for reliable results. An urts is anything but draft-free. It's not just a question of applying the test to one or two individual animals. It's the herd that counts. For this situation all the reindeer that belong to the Tsaatan are basically one unit. From time to time groups mix, especially if families join to make a camp with several urts. The reindeer graze together. When their calves are born, the associated fluids are spread on the ground. If an animal is infected, those fluids will carry the organism that can then be ingested as others graze nearby. It can persist on the ground for long periods. If an infected female is a first-time mother, the calf may well be born dead and will likely be riddled with the brucella organisms. The risk to other herd members increases as the little corpse may lie on the ground for days and herd members graze nearby.

While this is the number one way that the disease can be spread from one animal to another, the main risk for people is via the drinking of unpasteurized milk. Pasteurization is hardly an option in the taiga, so the milk must be boiled to make sure it is safe.

Two herders walked over to the small group of reindeer, tended by a small boy, who was standing near the urts. A minute later, holding it by the halter, they led the first one to my station near the urts. As the men held it, I collected blood from the jugular vein. The whole thing took less than a minute. It was in stark contrast to the process we'd used in Finland. There were no handling yards, chute, and no board under its belly. The cow was standing in the open, seemingly without a care in the world. Binde stood by with the rack in which to place the tubes. We were under way.

While I'd told Morgan about the card test and its usefulness in fieldwork, she had not seen it in action and did not know how it works. Nansalmaa sat next to her.

For the test I needed to use the pipettes to extract the pale golden serum in the glass tubes sitting above the dark lump of clotted blood. Because we could not freeze the samples and take them back to a lab we had to do the tests right away. If not frozen, the serum would rapidly deteriorate and the results in UB would be meaningless. Unfrozen serum is a great medium to grow all sorts of things.

Nansalmaa's English is good, so I didn't need Binde to translate. A bevy of children look on as we started.

I pointed to the ten pear-shaped spaces, each three centimetres from top to bottom, on the card. "We need to put two tiny drops of the stain at the widest part of each space. Then we take a drop of serum and plop it beneath the purple ones and stir them together. The first two come from the kit and are the benchmarks. Number one will look like a purple version of curdled milk (*agglutinated* is the Sunday name). It's the positive because the serum comes from an infected cow. Number two is from an animal known to be negative and will be clear."

On the very first card there was one test site with small clots, so it was perfect to explain everything. By the time we'd finished with the last card one more was positive. Two out of 32 is a lot. Even the slightest agglutination means a positive, but had the temperature and drafts affected the interpretation?

The best thing about this situation was that we could explain the test and the results to all the folks in the camp right away. Morgan told me that it was the first time that anyone had demonstrated to the herders the results of any test.

There was not enough time to reach the next camp. We sorted our own bags and moved inside to "enjoy" another meal of ramen noodles. They may be nutritious, but they are certainly not my granny's steak and kidney pie.

The conversations, in a mix of English and Mongolian, circled round the tent. It was time for me to crawl into my sleeping bag. I drifted off as the light began to fade. Again, I've no idea how long the chatter carried on. It hardly mattered.

Next thing I knew was the sound of water pouring into a dish and the crackling of a fire in the stove. After more noodles, we were soon on our way. There was no hesitation about our direction. It was obvious that Ganbat and Borkhuu knew the location of every camp.

CHAPTER 15

Further into the East Taiga

At just past midday we reached a wide plateau covered in short-stemmed plants and scattered patches of gray and white rocks. A variety of heather-like shrubs, none of which I recognized, none more than 60 centimetres tall, covered most of the slope below. Small patches of a spiky grass and a few stunted trees made up the rest. The main colours were the russet and range of greens of the shrubs, some topped by tiny white flowers.

We crested a ridge where Nansalmaa and Binde stopped. I rode up alongside. The view all round showed snow on distant mountain peaks glistening in the sun. Lower ridges, too numerous to count, took up the middle ground. Each covered in a dark green blanket of trees. The steep slope fell away over 60 metres to a mix of trees, shrubs and grass.

Nansalmaa pointed at some small lakes on the valley floor away to our left. In the mid-afternoon sun they shone like little silver plates. I guessed them to be about two kilometres off. I nodded and started to look away when she said, "Doctor Jerry, see the urts."

"What?"

At this moment Morgan pulled up alongside. "That's the camp," she said, pointing at some minute white dots near the lakes. "You can see about nine urts."

Now I saw them. We got off our horses and led them as we zigzagged down to the valley floor where we remounted near a spring that fed a small stream headed towards the camp. After about a kilometre a reindeer grazed near the water.

Pretty soon others came into view and to our right a boy threw a saddle blanket onto a dark gray male, clambered up on its back, grabbed the hide halter and set off towards camp.

Within a hundred metres there were reindeer all around us. Some drinking from the stream, others grazing. Like kids everywhere, children played. If my own water games at that age involved folded paper turned into little boats, skipping stones or Pooh-sticks under bridges, who knows what these youngsters were up to? I'm sure they were having just as much fun.

All the reindeer wore some kind of halter. Two of them were tied with heads close together, presumably as some sort of training device to stop them from wandering. They seemed to be not quite coordinated.

The scene reminded me of an unusual set of stocks on display in the small so-called criminal museum in the town of Rothenburg in Germany. They were neck stocks, called *Schandgeige*, consisting of a pair of joined wooden boards each with recessed half-moon rings set close together. At each end padlocks closed the boards. The half-moons became two circles not more than 30 centimetres apart. The German stocks were specifically designed, according to the plaque, for quarrelling people, usually two women, but also married couples. If the two could not get on, and their bickering disturbed the citizens, they would be sentenced to a period in the stocks, literally cheek by jowl. They had to cooperate in everything. *Everything.*

Life might be a bit easier for these two reindeer. They only had to agree on direction, and if one wanted to lower its head to graze, the other had to at least bend at the neck.

As we got near the camp, I saw several urts scattered on flat ground. Most surrounded by a post and rail fence. One such fence did not protect an urts but a tall radio mast. Binde explained, "This is the autumn camp for several families. We are very close to the border with Russia. They can contact Tsagaan Nuur or other soum centres if they need to. They can also listen to news."

We tied our horses to rails and dismounted. I looked around and realized that, although we were in a remote mountain valley with none of the mod cons we are used to in Canada, we were not back in another century. Standing next to an unfenced urts was a large satellite dish with a cable running under the canvas into the tent. Leaning against the wall near the south-facing door stood a solar panel.

Binde said, "This allows the family to watch programs on their little televisions. The favourite shows are subtitled Korean soap operas."

An attractive motherly woman appeared from an urts and came over to greet us, with a big smile for Morgan. She said something and Binde at once translated to explain that our hostess saw us coming down the hillside and had started a brew.

We sat and I remembered to try to avoid pointing my feet at the fire or at others in the room. This wasn't as easy as I hoped. Recent knee trouble that led to some cartilage removal made bending awkward and squatting impossible. Sitting sideways was the only solution. I made sure my hat was correctly set down.

An old hand-crank sewing machine covered in a protective cloth sat among the household goods. On the west side, where we visitors would sleep, bedding was piled up against the base of the tent walls. Some cured reindeer hides and a few soft bags of what I guessed to be personal clothing were stacked there as well. We were invited to add our own backpacks to that area to enhance the draught-proofing. There were too many of us to crowd into the urts for the night and without any discussion our three local men later slept in a different urts.

It was tea time again. The wok was soon empty of tea as I loosened up after another long day in the saddle. As soon as we all had our drinks (happily salt-free), our hostess started to make those delicious chapatis. Two filled the cavity in my stomach.

I had been in tipi-like structures before, both at home in Saskatoon and many years ago as a Boy Scout in England. That first tipi has stuck in my memory for many years. It had been imported from the United States by the school headmaster, Mr. Cooper, and was only used once a year at the summer camp we went to for ten days. It was decorated with geometric designs all around the outside. I suppose, with the benefit of hindsight and Google, it must have been made to match the patterns of one or more of the plains nations such as the Cheyenne, Sioux, Arapaho or Kiowa. At camp, far up the valley known as Nethercombe, in the beautiful Quantock Hills of Somerset, Mr. Cooper and the other scout leaders slept in it and we boys gathered there in the evenings for hot chocolate, singalongs and stories.

As we chatted, I heard the clicking of reindeer feet, which sounds like castanets being struck out of synch, and the gentle cough-like calls of the calves as they came into camp. A group of about 50, accompanied by two young women, both up on white deer, were coming into camp. The herding scene was a striking example of the degree of tameness of these animals compared to the ones I know of in Alaska, where a helicopter is often used to drive a herd, or elsewhere where snowmobiles are used for the same purpose.

I'd not realized they were soon to be tethered for the night. We stood and watched them as the teenagers tied each by short lengths of rope or rawhide to stakes driven into the turf or tree trunks laid out on the ground. Each animal was separated far enough from its neighbour to ensure that the ropes didn't get tangled. I soon learned that the tethering has other sound purposes.

First, the calves are held away from their dams. This prevents them from sucking and so allows the owners to milk the cows in the morning. After that essential task is done, the calves are allowed to join their mothers and they all leave for the day.

There's a second sound reason for holding the animals near to camp. Nighttime restraint prevents them from wandering because the wolves that roam the mountains would not hesitate to hunt them down.

Folks emerged from another urts and headed towards the one we were in. A meeting was about to take place. Morgan asked me to talk about the technology and potential of artificial insemination.

Following the Russian-driven collectivization, the numbers had not rebounded after the people's return to the taiga. As Binde put it, the herders were concerned about breeding problems. Among them was that wild reindeer sometimes bred their tame deer. "If that happens, the calves are too wild to fit into the herd."

Morgan expanded on our previous discussions. "Their own animals have become so quiet over the long years of history that goes back who knows how long that the wild blood means the new ones are too difficult to handle and so don't become tame. The other worry is that there are not enough bulls, usually one or two per camp. Some matings are between closely related herd members. Father x daughter and even that daughter's daughter, brother x sister, son — mother and so on. They have expressed interest in the possibility of getting new genes into the population from outside."

As far as I'm concerned, semen collection and freezing from other deer species is no big deal. The protocols are very similar to the ones developed for cattle. Reindeer semen collection is not much different. As Morgan knew, one of my clients in Saskatchewan, Norm Mitchell, already had some stored in liquid nitrogen.

We also needed to discuss issues about the type of reindeer from which semen could be obtained. The Tsaatan deer are used for milking and riding.

With explanations, a diagram of the reproductive tract and the process, I tried to convey the technical side and we discussed the subject in some detail. Questions that I tried to answer came up.

Finally, with night setting in, and our shadows dancing on the canvas behind us, the others headed back home, and we crawled into our sleeping bags.

With the canvas walls filtering the dawn light, I was awake at six o'clock as is my habit. I lay and thought for a while about home and my comfy bed that contrasted with the undulations of the ground under my mattress. I soon left the cozy sleeping bag, crept out of the urts (trying not to wake anyone else), rubbed my eyes to clear the sleepy dust and wandered round the camp where the reindeer were tethered. With the temperature only a few degrees above freezing, their breath created little wisps of moisture.

The morning rituals done, a bowl of tea gave that warm and welcome feeling.

Now to work. The blood samples were collected and processed. The mixture of fluids in one of the funny-face compartments on the cards was clumped.

Most of the herd was released to graze. A few were kept back. One of these was at once roped down and turned on her back for me to examine. It was easy to see why. The udder was raw and red, covered in a mass of nasty-looking inflamed sores. Were these fresher versions of the ones we saw on Aruna's cow? Or were they caused by something different? I never found out the cause. The purple permanganate and zinc oxide salve could once more reduce pain. We walked over to where folks of all ages were chatting.

Tsend, a blind Elder whom Morgan told me is a shaman, walked hand in hand with her little granddaughter. The child wanted to be lifted onto a deer. Morgan explained that each child is given a white reindeer at birth. The old lady stood proudly next to the little girl's totem. Binde and Jason did the honours while we snapped a few pictures. Nearby a young couple were both holding a small child, perhaps a year old, on the back of yet another white animal.

It was obvious the two little scenes were for our benefit. Similar "show-and-tell" events occur in most cultures. Social media platforms are the latest form.

Back in the urts, after another welcome bowl of tea, I delved into my day pack. The pipe cleaners emerged again. I twisted four red ones into make-believe spectacles and wiggled them over a little girl's ears. Next came two red barrettes for her hair. She held her doll, obviously a gift from some previous visitor, and turned for a photo. Her eyes opened wide when I showed her the image on the back of the camera. She held her breath for a moment then turned to her mother as a grin lit up her face.

By noon the work was finished. Time to mount up and move on.

In the next camp came a surprise. Half the deer had bits of red, yellow, blue and clear plastic bags tied to their antlers. A simple answer by Borkhuu to a question provided the answer. "They are deterrents. Tourists take photos of the camps and the reindeer without asking permission." Plastic bags on heads aren't much of a memento.

Two camps later we finished our visit to the east taiga. The brucella card test continued to come up positive on a few of the compartments. I'd not been keeping track of our route and was pleasantly surprised to arrive back at the starting ger by early afternoon where the two little girls carrying the water-filled milk churn had been.

Long before dusk we'd crossed the river and were back at the inn.

CHAPTER 16

Off West

The lake shimmered in the morning sun as the fireball rose above the snow-tipped peaks. The glassy surface of the lake meant that those peaks appeared twice, only a thin dark line between the upper jagged row and their mirror images.

With eyes almost shut against the glare, I could just see the splash of the five of diamonds spinning lure land out almost 40 metres away. Once more I reeled in, hoping to catch a breakfast treat, perhaps a half-kilo, trout-like lenok, with actual taste as opposed to the flavourless noodles we had been eating.

No luck.

As I headed back to the inn, I saw a woman squatted at the lake's edge to fill water containers and a man nearby gazing towards the mountains next to a dun-coloured horse.

After replenishing the syringes and other bits and pieces of veterinary equipment, rolling up my sleeping bag and putting on my red Gortex jacket and my much battered felt hat, I headed out the inn's door and shoved the gear into the van alongside the other folks' bags.

We were heading to the Barone taiga, west of the village. Morgan told me that this time there were no bridges to cross or a ferry. The grass-covered track ran almost straight for half an hour, ending in a semi-circular ring of golden-coloured larches. Gala came to a stop at the edge of the forest. Bayanmunk, Ganbat and Borkhuu were there, squatting beside the same dozen horses that had been our transport for our time in the east.

We piled out of the cramped van and sat while the men tightened the girths of all of them. Bayanmunk took a quick look at me, perhaps to assure me that this time there would be no slippage.

As we rested, waiting for the gear to be lashed to the pack horse saddles, I saw a man away to my right, using a scythe to cut the tall grass up the slope. He was making hay with the grass that was starting to turn from summer green to autumn brown.

In a flash I was 10 years old, watching Bill Wallace, "Old Bill" as we kids knew him, the lean, grizzled handyman on my granny's farm in England's Isle of Wight. He was using his scythe to cut the edges of lanes and the wheat too close to the hedges where the reaper-binder couldn't go. I can still see his metronomic swings, back and forth, back and forth, a single step forward at each swing. Every now and again he pulled a honing stone from the holster on his belt. With a few economical strokes he put back the fine edge of the long blade.

It was quickly back to reality. We mounted up and headed into the trees.

We had not been riding for more than ten minutes when Ganbat turned towards some bushes loaded with dark purple berries that looked just like the Saskatoon berries of home. I plucked a few higher ones and found them just as juicy and delicious as those we pick early on July mornings. The best way to enjoy ours is to go straight back to the house for breakfast, make pancakes and spread the berries, pour on some maple syrup and top the already mouth-watering treat with a generous spoonful of whipped cream, as we sit on the deck and enjoy the crisp smells of cool morning air.

We emerged from the trees onto a grassy plateau that stretched away to another tree stand in the distance. Another plain and a couple of valleys and by late morning we arrived at a single urts. A man of uncertain age, by the look of his lined face at least 60, came out to greet us. Binde told me that this was Ghosta, the most important shaman of the entire Tsaatan People. He was holding a little girl, her blond hair tied in pretty pink ribbons. He put her down and slipped her trousers to her knees. Then a surprise. The child peed. A boy, with a penis! (I'm not imagining, I have seen one before.) A much younger woman squatted at the tent door holding a tiny infant on her lap.

Binde explained: "Parents do not cut the hair of any children until they are 3. The boy children wear these ribbons just like the girls. The disguise protects the boys to that age so that evil spirits will not take them. Then they undergo the hair ceremony and are recognized as boys."

It all depends upon your belief base. There is clear evidence in Western medicine that infant mortality rates are greater in boys than in girls. There are zero chances that a nomadic reindeer herder will be familiar with the publications of the data. Observation and long-accumulated cultural knowledge will have led to the same conclusion long before modern scientists made statistical studies. The Tsaatan solution is easy to explain.

We exchanged the formal "Sain baina uu?" The locals chatted for a while when Binde turned to me.

"Ghosta is asking you to look at an injured reindeer. He wants to know if you can do anything for it."

Sadly, the condition was beyond my help. The animal had a damaged hip. He'd slipped on some rocks. The problem was that it wouldn't be able to make any kind of trek to a new spot when

Ghosta and his wife moved camp, something they would soon do, riding other reindeer.

Another of Ghosta's herd had a swollen joint. It might have been due to an injury of some sort. However, it is also a consequence of brucellosis in many species including caribou and bison in Canada, Cape Buffalo and other African hoofstock, both cattle and wild. It was the fourth we'd seen. In the hope of obtaining a sample of the fluid to find out if it contained the brucella bacterium meant a shave, some alcohol to clean and sterilize the skin and then a syringe to draw out some fluid and transfer it to a tube. Again the lack of ice for transport to the lab was a concern, but it was worth a try.

I didn't find out if Ghosta's injured deer moved with the family or ended up in the pot. Morgan told me the Tsaatan seldom eat their animals. The females supply milk that was once the main source of most nutrients. For other protein the men hunt for wild animals, preferring wapiti and moose above all else, but are willing to take whatever they see.

We had to move on. The quickest route to the next camp was straight ahead over the ridge in front of us. Halfway up the steep climb we all dismounted to lead our horses through the trees. We needed to take a breather at the top.

From the larch woods we rode steadily west. Bayanmunk started a long song that, to my ears, sounded like a mourning dirge.

At the top of another tree-covered ridge we saw, down in a wide valley, a camp. There were three urts set some 50 metres apart among stunted spruce trees. The first person to greet us was Erdenchimeg. Beside her, hiding shyly, were two little girls. As I now knew well, the first order of business was that welcome bowl of tea.

At the back of the tent, hanging on a pole, a twisted knot dangled down. "What's the significance of that?" I asked. "I've seen one in every urts so far."

"It's an endless knot," replied Binde. "Called an *Ulzii*. It brings good fortune or blessing. It ensures strength and long life."

After a decent interval, we got to work. With my sampling equipment laid out I was soon collecting blood from each deer's jugular vein while Borkhuu or Ganbat held the halters. This time there were no positives.

After this part of our task was completed, Erdenchimeg asked me to examine one of her cows. High up on its back some yellow pus oozed through the hair. Was this a saddle sore, maybe from a badly placed packsaddle?

I asked her about this possibility. She looked at Binde and was obviously nodding yes. But, as Binde translated, she added, "It has not been able to carry anything for a long time. We cannot even ride her. She has no milk and has not had a calf for two years."

Nansalmaa again squirted some of her favourite potassium permanganate on the area. To me it didn't look as if this would do any good at all, so I decided a closer examination was a must. The most satisfactory way to do this was to lay the reindeer on her side and probe the wound. There was no need for the rope pull method for cows we had shared at Aruna's camp. Borkhuu and Ganbat simply hobbled her and laid her down.

After boiling up some instruments, I made a careful examination by inserting a pair of forceps into the wound. There was a nasty surprise. It was not superficial. The instrument went straight down some ten centimetres when the tip stopped against bone. That's not all. Something solid in the space moved a little, which made me suspect I was dealing with a serious condition. Had a foreign body entered the cavity by accident? It seemed unlikely. When I pulled out the forceps, they were coated with the same yellow pus.

I put the forceps back in and tried to grasp the moving object and pull it up. It was all too easy. A ten-centimetre length of bone, grasped between the jaws of the forceps, emerged. Its bottom end was rotten. I'd removed the top end of one of the spinous processes of a vertebra, likely one of the first two of the backbone just beyond those seven of the neck. If the end I was looking at was rotten, so was the vertebra of which it was a part.

How to put this finding in terms that Erdenchimeg could understand and accept?

I told her that, even in the best hospital in the world, there could be no successful treatment. It would be impossible to clean out the abscess and hope for a cure.

I asked her if she'd seen one of her animals with this sort of condition before. When she answered yes, my task became much simpler. She'd had one the previous year and, as she put it, when she opened the body, the pus had gone right round the spine and appeared in the chest. The bone of the spine had more-or-less rotted away.

She accepted the diagnosis and information with equanimity. We also discussed the problem with heavy packs and the saddle.

It was time to break out the sleeping bags and the ramen noodles. Oh joy!

When I stepped out of the urts in the morning, the first thing I saw was our hostess crouched beside a deer as she milked it. She would use the milk to add to tea and making curds and cheese. Her littlest daughter stood nearby, munching on something. A brief movie clip joined others in my camera.

After visits to two more camps, more blood sample collection and two more cows with the pox-like lesions on the udders, I totted up the number we'd seen of this condition, something Nansalmaa had seen for the first time in Ghosta's herd two months before our arrival. She had seen ten cases in July; we saw a further 23. The condition, whatever its cause, is obviously contagious.

We headed back to Tsagaan Nuur and thence to Murun in the Forgan van. Next morning we climbed into the ancient Antonov and winged back to the capital.

The highlight of the last evening in UB was to join Lil on a visit to a jazz club. The group leader at once invited her to come up and join the band. He obviously knew her talents. The glorious tones of her flute blended seamlessly into the sounds of trumpet, clarinet, trombone and riffs of the drum kit.

CHAPTER 17

A Second Year

A key objective for the 2005 trip was to get a clearer picture of the status of the Tsaatan reindeer.

Dr. Paul Stevens, a faculty member at the University of Saskatchewan, who headed up the successful Training for Rural Development program in Mongolia, had learned of the program and called when I returned in 2004. We chatted and he offered funding if I could go beyond just the reindeer studies and meet with scientists at the Mongolian State University of Agriculture (MSUA) to talk not only about the reindeer but also describe our work in the field of game farming. He also suggested a meeting with rural veterinarians to cover the subject of AI as a means to improve the overall performance of livestock, especially cattle. This was a no-brainer. It would just be a question of getting to Ulaanbaatar a day or two before heading to the taiga.

For the reindeer work I needed to do a few things. The first was tied to obtaining DNA from the reindeer. If we could get some, we could answer questions about genetics and disease with a single sample split in two. Only a minute amount of the material is needed for analysis, so samples can be sent to different labs.

I'd been in contact with Dr. Knut Røed at the Norwegian School of Veterinary Science who had extensive experience with reindeer DNA. He wrote he'd be delighted to help figure out more about the genetic relationship of the Tsaatan reindeer with other herds across Eurasia.

On the disease front, Nansalmaa was concerned about one condition in particular. She had a strong suspicion the deer have anaplasmosis, a condition caused by a bacterium that can be found in red blood cells. Under the microscope she had seen the characteristic darkly stained organism in blood smears, but that can do no more than give a clue. It cannot provide proof. To confirm Nansalmaa's suspicion, we needed DNA, and the second portion of the split samples would enable us to determine which of several types it was.

We could run tests for disease in the lab of my colleague Dr. Janet Hill, whose lab is in the Department of Microbiology at the vet college in Saskatoon. There was no equipment or trained skilled technician in UB able to extract this material. The challenge was to seek a person with the technical know-how and the willingness to travel to a distant land.

From my Saskatoon office I had a suspicion that there might be someone right in the city who had the skills. A phone call, followed later by a 500-metre walk, got me to the office of Dr. Yves Plante, head of the Saskatchewan Research Council. He had put the word out and learned that Vicki Gerwing, a technician with an adventurous spirit, who worked in his lab, was excited and interested at the chance to go to Mongolia.

As usual it all came down to funding. We needed at least $5,000. Morgan knew the value of a well-presented proposal only too well. Her efforts through Itgel covered some of the costs. The charitable organization Veterinarians Without Borders generously provided the balance of the travel expenses. Dr. Plante allowed Vicki to bring the supplies needed. It all added up to enough money to send Vicki to the veterinary school in UB, where she could work in the lab run by Dr. Janchivdor Erdenebaatar.

The blood samples we would bring back from Tsagaan Nuur could never be imported into Canada because of the potential transmission of any of several kinds of disease, especially foot-and-mouth disease that occurs in Mongolia. It can spread among cattle and sheep like wildfire and have disastrous effects on a country's economy. In 1951–1952 just such an outbreak occurred in Saskatchewan when an immigrant from Europe arrived with some sausage. DNA is inert so can be safely brought back to Canada for analysis.

A third task was to follow up on last year's field results. We had collected 30 fecal samples and examined them at the vet school lab in UB. It was a simple matter to add bottles of deworming injection, the one that Dr. Soveri and the team he worked with in Finland had studied, which proved to be highly effective. It was just a case of adding several bottles to my kit, enough to treat every animal we encountered.

Then it was off on that arduous, jetlag-inducing, four-airport trip. This year the local contact person was Tsegi, who met me at the airport. The taxi took us to a hotel, rather than the apartment Morgan had rented. Next day we got to the veterinary school, which is part of the MSUA, and met with Dr. Erdenebaatar and the general manager of the research institute and his colleagues.

The latter were clearly interested in the potential of AI of the reindeer and particularly impressed that we already had semen stored in liquid nitrogen at home. Before the discussion could proceed, I emphasized that we needed verification by DNA sampling of the suitability of crossing Canadian reindeer genes with

Mongolian ones. Tsegi agreed to set up the meeting with the rural vets when I returned from the taiga.

Two days later, the Itgel team arrived at the apartment Morgan had rented. There was no Lil, which was a surprise given the role she had played in the foundation of Itgel. No Jason either. Instead there were two new team members, both volunteers who had connections with Morgan through her Colorado base. Dynamic, ever-smiling Bill Coyle had come in as a volunteer from Denver, where he ran a lawn turf business. His cheerful open face and ready grin were instantly welcoming. Morgan said that we would later meet up with the other volunteer, student Meagan Flenniken, who knew Bill through family connections. We also met the new translator, a young man called Byamba. He was bright and fluent, and we soon found out he had a ready wit.

As soon as I could I went shopping for a del with Byamba. Last year it had quickly become obvious there is nothing like a del as a basic garment when riding a horse. It covers both upper body and legs. It's windproof. All the rural Mongolians we met had worn them when outside. Byamba explained that dels are available with two insulating levels, mainly summer and winter, as well as fancy or functional. I jammed my thick gray one into the now fully stuffed hockey bag.

The Chinggis Khan restaurant where I'd had my first ever meal in the country, and taken a moment to decipher the typo-filled menu, had gone. So worrying how my eggs were sourced was not a concern.

At Tsagaan Nuur we caught up with Meagan, who brought gentle charm and an inquisitive mind to the team. She told me she was considering a career in veterinary medicine and when she'd heard from Bill about the work she'd at once volunteered to join up. Her task was to carry out studies to find out what the reindeer eat and also collect specimens of those items for identification.

We once more started in the east taiga.

My new del, with its bright-yellow cloth boos, proved to be ideal. The coat's skirt reached well below my knees, with enough cloth to cover my legs and keep them warm. The top half was the clever bit. The flap across the chest, held in place with a toggle on the shoulder, created a huge pocket for keeping a snack warm, storing samples and who knows what else. I somehow doubt the sample property had been in the minds of those who designed the garment.

This time we avoided the swamp where I sank last year. Aruna had moved her camp no more than a kilometre down the valley. This time there were two other urts nearby. All three stood only 100 metres from the stream we crossed last year.

Beside the dwellings a herd of reindeer stood tethered to logs. The cattle we saw last year were also lying about. She told me that the cow with the sore udder had recovered. I'm not sure how Aruna would manage to ensure that her two herds could find food, as the ground within a hundred or so metres was 90 per cent rocks. Reindeer and cattle have very different dietary needs, so she'd set up where both could easily move to suitable sources, the reindeer north, the cattle south.

We collected and tested yet more reindeer blood. The joints of two were swollen, one in the "knee" of a front leg, the other low down on the hindmost. My curiosity about the swellings peaked. Were they all due to trauma? Possible, but three so far?

The horses were loaded, and we thanked our hostess before heading downstream along the wide valley. There the creek joined an even wider bed of rocks with three shallow streams coalescing and separating again, gurgling away to our right.

The familiar bubbling sound of water tumbling over stones triggered an instant flashback. I saw myself, rod in hand, standing below a cataract on the Nanyuki River below our house in Kenya, as my line snaked out, a Royal Coachman at the end of the leader, towards a spot where a trout had just risen.

Back to reality. We crossed the stream. Here the horses splashed through, the water barely covering their hooves.

A well-worn track meandered through the brush beside the water.

The golden colours of larches across the stream contrasted with the dark green of the pines and the reds and yellows of early autumn leaves on low bushes. The skyline changed to snow-capped mountains that peeked out shyly in the distance beyond rounded hills.

The reindeer work continued much as in 2004, but with a few interesting differences.

At our next camp our team was invited to split and sleep in different urts. I was the single guest of JBat, the only person I had so far met wearing glasses. He too had a solar panel dangling on the south side of his "mobile home." Although we shared no more than ten words of the same language, I soon discovered his charm and wit. By gestures and grins we shared parts of each other's lives.

While I parked on a nearby log, JBat opened up the newspaper that Byamba brought along. Rather than sit around doing nothing, I lifted his axe to help split some logs for the fire. A glance at the axe head revealed there is more than one way to wedge the handle into the metal. He'd jammed five used rifle bullet cases into the space, evidence of hunting and an unusual example of recycling.

Our last stop in the east taiga brought a pleasant surprise. We'd arrived where Ganbat's family lived with the reindeer. As we sat around the urts, his wife, Khurlee, produced another of those delicious, giant, bagel-shaped, sourdough loaves.

Now we turned back and made our way to the ger with its gorgeous door where Gala was waiting for us. The little girls were playing outside and took little notice of us.

We were all looking forward to the new luxury in town. A smart resident had extended the side of a house and installed two shower cubicles. Here was the chance for a proper cleanup after days in the mountains. A face cloth and soap mixed with mountain-fed stream water was the perfect antidote to what was probably not the most delightful body odour. It was pay in advance for a bucket of hot water to be poured into an overhead tub. A pull of a lever. Instant joy.

Next morning we headed west. Once more Gala drove up the valley to the edge of the trees where Bayanmunk, Borkhuu and Ganbat were waiting with the horses. We headed up through the trees and onto the plateau.

Two hours later we dipped down into a valley and reached Ghosta's camp. There were more reindeer to sample. The one with the damaged hip was not among them.

From there we went up the valley for a while and then turned, went over a grassy ridge and dropped into a wide valley where Erdenchimeg greeted us. She confirmed she did slaughter the animal that had the horrible abscess on its spine last year. And, yes, the backbone was rotten.

We arrived late in the afternoon at the next camp, too late to do any work. We took it easy and enjoyed meeting the families.

A few pipe cleaners emerged once again from my day pack. Inquisitive small children tried to figure them out. A mischievous boy caught on right away. With a big grin, he showed off his creations. He was wearing pipe-cleaner glasses and holding up a black and white creature with a long neck. A dragon?

Next morning it was off again, along a stream, past another group of deer as we headed towards the neck of the valley.

CHAPTER 18

A Shaman's Treatment

As we climbed, the trees became scattered and stunted. A lone larch, golden in its autumn colours, signalled the top of the tree-line. We crested a ridge and there below us were rocks that varied in size from soccer ball to dishwasher. After a rest for both horses and humans, Bayanmunk pointed with his chin down the slope to the valley. He advised me to let go the reins and tie them up so the horse wouldn't get caught up in them. The horse picked its own way without hesitation. He'd done it all before.

The valley curved gently to the right and then the camp came slowly into view. A small number of stunted larch trees had somehow grown roots and survived. We collected blood from the few animals that were already tethered. Bill Coyle had taken on the task of administering all the deworming injections. Then it was time for more ramen noodles, some storytelling and sleep.

As usual, like many men of my age, the urgent need to get up early to check if my kidneys had done their job overnight had at once to be dealt with. I emerged through the tent flap to a land-scape that looked as if it had been dusted with icing sugar. The entire tethered herd stood quietly among the orange-coloured larches and the shrubs that had long since lost their leaves. Just visible through mist-like falling snow, the steep slope at the head of the valley looked fuzzy, as if seen through a plastic curtain.

I turned and saw Bill, holding his satellite phone to his ear, a grimace on his face because of the cold. When he clicked it off, he explained he was calling home to Colorado to change the sprinkler settings on his turf business. I'd no idea that one could do that remotely, but he assured me he could do it at any time from anywhere.

The work continued, but I was having real difficulty with my part of the procedure. Over the last two days my right forearm, between my elbow and watch strap, had swelled to double its normal size. I had no idea why. I'd not hit it against a rock, I hadn't fall off the horse, but it was so sore I couldn't even hold my bowl of tea. That's serious for a guy almost weaned on the brew. Two doses of paracetamol had made no difference. When I told Byamba of it, he at once suggested a visit to Soyan, the shaman who lived in the adjacent urts.

The 103-year-old was sitting quietly. Byamba did the introductions and explanation for our visit. Before we got any further, the old lady said, "If that man has a bad knee, he can point his feet."

We were sitting across the urts from her, three metres away. Since last year's trip, I'd had more bits of cartilage (nicknamed "joint mice") removed from the joint, so obeying the protocol that requires no foot pointing was impossible. The white discs of Soyan's advanced cataracts were plain to see. She was virtually blind, so she could only have figured out my problem by hearing my specific shuffling.

After a few minutes of discussion, she called me over and ran her gnarled hand up and down my arm and bent the elbow. Without further ado, she reached behind her, pulled out three fleshy leaves, each about 20 centimetres across, and told me to heat them up on the stove a few times in the night and wrap them around the painful area.

When we returned to our sleeping quarters, Byamba asked our hostess if she would let us put the leaves on the stove. They were difficult to hold in place on the swollen area, so from my first aid kit I took a purple bandage and covered the warm leaves in place so I could freely move the arm to prevent the remedy falling on the floor. Our hostess reached behind her and grabbed several reindeer hides, covered in their winter hair. She must have seen me as "the Elder," or perhaps took pity on me. In any case, my comfort level increased enormously with the super-soft mattress, as luxurious as any commercial one. One hide is good enough for a reindeer living in the frozen north. Three hides was sheer hedonism, but then a moderate amount of hedonism every now and again is okay.

By morning my arm was back to normal. The swelling had vanished. Holding that dawn's kick-starter bowl of tea was no problem. I suggested to Byamba that we go back to the old lady and thank her. It turned out to be more than thanks as we began a lengthy conversation. I knew that Soyan's daughter is the blind shaman Tseren we'd met the previous year. There was more. Byamba told me that her grandson is Ganbat, our veterinary technician. The parallels between our families were obvious. I told her that my wife and son are doctors and I am a vet. Next thing I knew, I was invited to sit by the old lady and Byamba clicked the shutter.

When I asked Byamba to find out the name of the special leaves, he shook his head. "I can't ask that." It must be a shaman secret. The cause of the swollen arm remains a mystery, but the relief was the thing that counted.

Over the next ridge we entered a camp where several urts stood, not far from a small stream running at the base of a steep slope with moss-covered rocks jumbled up like collapsed Lego pieces. As we all enjoyed the welcome bowl of tea, the clicking of reindeer feet just outside the urts grew louder.

With our work done, the deworming injections given and blood samples collected, it was time to head back to base.

We left the camp, climbing the steep slope in a new direction. At the crest, not a tree in sight, we took a break. All dismounted for a breather. Down and up again, over the next ridge, now well above the treeline, we came across a snow-covered ovoo. This one told a new tale.

A few sticks formed the rough pyramid. With no trees in sight, every stick must have been carried up. Near the top of the tallest one, a small, carved helicopter was attached with some twine. Obviously, we'd crested at a pass for choppers that cross the mountains. As at the previous ovoo, Bayanmunk led our circling of the important structure.

On the way back to Tsagaan Nuur we stopped at another spring. This one more developed than the one we saw last year. The tumbling water was directed, at waist height, into a cubicle built of split logs. Coming straight out of the mountainside, the water was a tad nippy, to say the least. Borkhuu told us this is an important site for treatment of bad backs. Two minutes with the near-icicle water cascading onto anyone's back would anesthetize it for a considerable length of time. Bad back? No way.

On the way back to Murun, we diverted to a camp where some of Nansalmaa's relations lived and owned livestock. Here they were cattle. Also the family lived in gers, not urts. I was asked to take a look at a horse with a sore low down on its neck.

It looked very much like a case of something I'd never seen before, but the pictures in my textbook from student days resurfaced like a Google search. It's called fistulous withers, a condition that is usually caused by an ill-fitting saddle anywhere on the spine and appears as pus in the middle line. This one was way too far forward to have been caused by a saddle.

Once more brucellosis was on any list of possible diagnoses. The condition is endemic in cattle herds across Mongolia, and in horses it can show up exactly as it appeared here. I'd never seen the condition in a horse — it had long been eliminated in the United Kingdom when I was at vet school — but it's still sporadically seen in some US states, especially Texas. Thank goodness my forceps only went in two centimetres. Not to the horrific ten-centimetre depth I'd seen in Erdenchimeg's reindeer.

Nansalmaa prepared another bowl of her pale purple permanganate solution, sprayed some on the area and daubed it with her zinc oxide paste. We headed on our way back to Tsagaan Nuur and, after that magic hot shower, on to Murun.

This year the Itgel budget did not include a return flight from Murun to UB. Bill, Meagan and I had no choice. We jammed ourselves into another Forgan van and headed southeast. The flight would have taken an hour. This drive, over the typical almost nonexistent roads, took a full day. At the end of our jolting trip that mountain spring therapy would have been just the thing, but it was far behind us.

The delay created a problem. A meeting with the rural vets, arranged for the day we were expected in UB, was no longer possible, although Tsegi had tried to alter the flight dates. We planned for next year.

There was time to deliver the chilled blood tubes to the vet college where Vicki waited to start her work in Dr. Erdenebaatar's lab. She had no trouble extracting the DNA. I packed up the material that posed no disease risks at all in Canada, or anywhere else, and headed home.

CHAPTER 19

Year Three in Mongolia

The Tsaatan reindeer work started much earlier than in previous years, and in Colorado not Mongolia. At Morgan's request, I attended the Reindeer Owners and Breeders Association conference in Parker to report on the work we'd done.

During the first evening's session, at the meet and greet, came a wonderful surprise. Two Mongolian musicians, both clothed in gorgeous dels, performed for us. A tall powerful man in a dark purple one sang a throat song just like the one I'd heard at the Children's Garden in 2004. His ability to intone two notes at once was just as puzzling as before. The seated man in a golden del played a short mysterious piece on his horse-head, two-string instrument.

Next day we got into the nuts and bolts of the reindeer industry. Disease control, reproduction, nutrition, marketing.

Tom Scheib, white hair, white beard and solid build, who would need only the red coat and hat to be Father Christmas himself in any parade, told of his experiences with reindeer and showed pictures of his harnessed reindeer pulling a decorated sled (with partly hidden wheels) in Macy's New York procession.

I had three time slots. The first was to report on the work we'd done, which I had to compress because I felt Morgan had gone way over her allotted half-hour. After many presentations and talks at scientific gatherings, I know one must stick to allotted times. Going over is discourteous to the organizers and the other speakers. I mentioned this problem to her, but the remark was not well received. Thus began what would become an uncomfortable time in the taiga.

My next task was to give a brief overview of the reproductive cycle of these fascinating animals, which boils down to season and day length. This is what I told them:

In spring and summer, while the cows are either heavily pregnant or fully engaged in raising their young, the bulls are infertile. The quality of the semen, what little of it there is, is so poor that sometimes there are no normal sperm cells visible under a microscope. Those that are there look like carcasses in an auto wrecker's yard. In late summer and early fall, heading into September, the level of the testosterone in their blood rises sharply in response to shortening day length. From almost too low to measure, the hormone levels rise several hundredfold in six weeks. The bulls change into violent, aggressive, raging sex maniacs. They want to gain control of a maximum number of females so as to breed and pass on their genes. Initially, they compete with faceoffs to show their antlers. The bigger, the better. Size does matter.

If there is no discernible difference between rivals, then the show and tell can get violent. Pushing and shoving may decide the winner. On rare occasions one of the combatants may score a telling blow and spear the other. That is often fatal. A much rarer occurrence is the interlocking of the complex branched antlers. If the lock cannot be undone, the two may soon perish of starvation or be easy targets for predators.

Meanwhile, the females are also gearing up for the fall breeding season. The adult hormones also start to cycle. In late September through to early November, the females come into heat. The bulls can readily detect the smell of such a cow and will make advances. She will not stand for him until she is good and ready. She needs to be at the right time in her cycle to have the best chance to conceive. As he gets more and more interested, she runs away, each time over shorter and shorter distances until she stands still. She is running away until she catches him.

On top of all this, the unique antler cycle of reindeer comes into play. They are the only member of the deer family in which both sexes carry the bony headgear.

Mature bulls drop their antlers once the breeding season is over, usually by Christmastime. After all, they are not much use for display purposes. During the rut they will have lost some 25 per cent of their body weight. The last thing they need is to hang on to a mass of now useless bone that weighs them down as they seek food to try and regain condition.

On the other hand, females do not cast theirs in winter. It gets even more complicated. Nonpregnant ones often cast in March or early April. If she is pregnant, her casting occurs around calving time in mid- to late May.

On the last afternoon of the meeting, Dr. Bob Dieterich, the man who chose not to take on the Itgel project before Morgan contacted me, chaired an "ask the experts" session. We did our best to answer a wide range of questions.

Back in Canada, an effort to get more funding to help with the project was successful. Veterinarians Without Borders again supported us with sufficient funds to bring Vicki back to Mongolia to continue the DNA extraction work. By adding this year's results to those of 2005 there'd be plenty of data to determine the genetic and disease status of the animals.

Dr. Paul Stevens, my University of Saskatchewan colleague, once more found funds for travel and we agreed that another meeting with vet college scientists and a trip to meet the rural vets would be a part of the journey.

At 8:00 the morning after my arrival in UB, through the jaded sleep of jetlag, I heard knocking, opened the apartment door and there stood a young woman named Ganimcheg. She'd been acting as in-country liaison for a different program run by Dr. Stevens while Tsegi, my previous contact, was in Canada. Almost without pause, Gana (as she asked to be called) told me to hurry and get dressed. She'd arranged for me to speak at the Mongolian University of Life Sciences in half an hour to welcome the incoming class of veterinary students.

Surprise and consternation! This would be a formal occasion. Normally, on any working field trips, my wardrobe would have been best described as adequate for the task at hand — scruffy jeans with reinforced knee patches fit for riding, long johns, three pairs of warm socks, T-shirts, a couple of old sweaters, waterproof pants and jacket, work gloves and, of course, my old felt hat. As luck would have it, I had arranged a storytelling gig in British Columbia on the way home. For that there was, in my luggage, my double-breasted dark blue blazer, a cravat and smart trousers.

A two-gulp swallow of milk and a grab of a couple slices of bread to have on the way was all the time we had before Gana bundled me into a waiting taxi.

The crowd of parents and family members were already standing outside the college. The array of smartly dressed older people, several in dazzling best dels, was an eye-opener. I was used to seeing the working ones of country folks. I was at once invited to join the dignitaries seated in front of the main doors of the university as they waited for the entertainment to start.

Down the steps between the pillars came four young couples; the men in tuxedos, the women in flowing red dresses trimmed with white. On the flat ground in front of the building they danced as one. They wheeled to a foxtrot then spun and stamped as the music changed seamlessly to a tango. The skirts swirled to the music.

A breakdancer spun and writhed like a coiled snake with rhythmic intensity and flipped backwards from shoulders to feet. I'm sure the rural parents had never seen such sights, but the applause was enthusiastic and long lasting.

From the seats, we moved up the steps in front of the building. The speeches, first by the university president Dr. Byamba, and then others, greeted the crowd (or so I assumed, given my Mongolian vocabulary).

My turn came. Gana translated. I recalled addresses to students from my own early university days and kept it short. The first task was to greet the new students, then congratulate and encourage them as they entered the next exciting phase of their lives. To the families, good wishes and more congratulations for the commitments they'd made in support of their children.

Then it was back to town and a stop at Chez Bernard for a proper breakfast — a cup of strong tea and a double helping of eggs Benedict. On top of the American accents, I heard something that sounded like a central Europe tongue, and then a Canadian from Ontario. We chatted briefly — he was on a trade mission.

Later that day, on a return to the university, came a meeting with faculty to follow up on last year's discussions about the possibility of AI of the reindeer in order to strengthen their possibly depleted gene pool. When the Mongolian colleagues heard the report of the DNA work carried out by Dr. Røed in Norway, and the complexity of the process in such a remote region, they expressed doubts about the feasibility and desirability of the endeavour.

We also discussed the disease situation and the problem of dealing with brucellosis. Now that we had a confirmed diagnosis of anaplasmosis, derived from the DNA work in Saskatoon, we developed a plan for treatment of sick animals and the supply of the correct antibiotic. Taking enough of the drug for this trip had been no problem. The bottles easily fit with the rest of the veterinary equipment in my blue and gray ex-hockey bag. The bigger issue was the "how" of ensuring that Ganbat and Borkhuu would be supplied with the drug for use in following years as needed.

Next day Gana took me to the town of Darkhan, Mongolia's second-largest city, to fulfill Paul Stevens's request for the session with the rural vets to discuss the techniques involved in AI, not only for reindeer but, in a more general sense, especially for cattle. Darkhan is a long way from the Hovsgol Mountains and the reindeer herding people. These folks were unlikely to get involved in that work, but Paul had told me of the strong interest in the subject of AI across Mongolia.

The first thing we saw as we entered the town was a huge statue of a mounted man playing his horse-head fiddle while his mount was at full gallop. The extraordinary work is a tribute to three important elements of Mongolian culture: the rider, the horse and the fiddle.

After two meetings it was off to Murun to catch up with the Itgel team. With one addition, Greg Finstad from Alaska, it was the same group as in 2005: Morgan, with a slightly frosty greeting; Bill Coyle; Meagan and Byamba. We all piled into the Forgan van. At first the trip to Tsagaan Nuur was routine, although a real treat was the sight of some beautiful demoiselle cranes, with their pale gray backs, eyeshadow-like black feathers on milk-white heads and black feather boas draped down the neck, that looked as if they were the models for vaudeville star Judy Garland, or a modern drag queen's outfit.

The trip turned to trouble after five hours. Gala chose a route across some soggy-looking ground. Within 15 metres we were going nowhere. A quick shift into the lowest of the gears merely helped the sinking feeling, as we were soon axle-deep in the mire. This being the steppes of Mongolia, we didn't expect a quick rescue. There was no automobile association with a tow truck to come to our aid.

We all piled out and start to shove. The result was a spray of black muck shooting back to hit those of us in direct line of the rear tires. Two hours later a man with a small flock of sheep came by, just as another Forgan appeared out of the blue. Gala asked for help, we hitched up the team, but the goop was more powerful than the hairy helpers.

Four hours later a khaki-coloured Forgan stopped near us (but not in the swampy ground). We hooked up his towing cable to ours, using my boos. The boos soon ripped apart and became useless as a belt for my del. The goop won again — we didn't move a centimetre.

We were now tired and hungry. Evening was drawing in. There was no food, not even ramen noodles, in the luggage. However, my day pack contained Saskatoon-bought comfort food, enough for the entire three weeks. A dozen Mars bars and a kilo of trail mix. A sacrifice was needed. Luckily, nobody had a nut allergy and we did have plenty of bottled water.

After a less than comfortable night, wrapped in sleeping bags to keep out the near-freezing cold, sitting or lounging in a crush of bodies, the atmosphere getting ever more pungent, we devoured the last of the trail mix.

Early next morning a small flock of sheep took no notice of us as their owner walked over to chat. He offered to walk back the 15 kilometres to Ulaan-Uul, the village we stopped at in 2004 when I was suffering from the after-effects of the tsoivan meal in the greasy spoon restaurant. He hoped the owner of a truck would be home. He left his sheep in our care.

Seven hours later the truck arrived. The Forgan was soon

squished out of the swampy ground and we were on our way. We'd been stuck for 22 hours.

After a restful night in Tsagaan Nuur, we set out to do our work. This time we started in the west taiga. Bayanmunk's home stood halfway to the jump-off point and he invited us in for a snack and to meet his family. Before we went into the house, I opened my big bag and took out the girth and leather bridle I'd purchased back home and gave them to him. It was a complete surprise to everyone. He lit up like a halogen lamp. There was no need for Byamba to translate his thank you.

In the warm room, as I sat by the stove, his wife offered a slice of bread heaped with clotted cream to go with my tea. Yesterday's dietary deprivation needed compensation. The hell with cholesterol excess! Yum! A great substitute comfort food, albeit not Mars bars and trail mix.

CHAPTER 20

Unexpected Encounters

Fortified by the snack, we piled back into the van. Twenty minutes later we were at the head of the valley where the harvest of hay had been scythed and stooked the previous year and the abrupt transition to trees had occurred.

At this point the uneasy atmosphere between Morgan and I that had started during the conference in Colorado began to deteriorate. I guess neither of us like being dictated to.

We mounted up and set off through the golden larches. We'd been going for less than an hour when we met another group crossing our path. The men were on horseback, their pack animals reindeer. They were travelling back from town with supplies and after a brief chat they headed off up a different trail than ours.

Fifteen minutes later, as we crested a small ridge and dropped down towards the stream, we saw two well-built log structures. Not the same ones that we'd seen before, but Byamba told me the water gushing into each from the uphill side is also considered to be therapeutic.

After visits to two more camps, we headed up beside a wide-ish river, about 30 metres across, its waters tumbling down from a lake.

Here was something quite new. Not only was this the largest camp I'd seen, with some 15 urts scattered among short spruce trees, but several of them were khaki-coloured. None of us, not even the Mongolians, had seen one before. On top of that, there were large, Western-style, ridge tents off to one side, near the edge of the lake, right where it narrowed above the rushing water.

A small group of Caucasians was standing next to a large reflector set up some three metres off the ground, while a man with his eye glued to a large movie camera bent over a tripod. A crew led by artist Gregory Colbert of *Ashes and Snow* was shooting another documentary, one of a series about the relationship between animals and people.

We were asked not to interfere with or take pictures of their work, but when a cameraman leant over to watch me examine a sick reindeer, and then fired off a few shots without asking my permission, I couldn't resist the opportunity to snap a few pictures of Sanjim, a local man, as he led a group of reindeer along the opposite side of the river and then wade in towards the film crew.

As he emerged, I noted he wore chest waders. Without them, the frigid water would have quickly soaked his clothes. It could also have led to hypothermia, never mind the rapid shrinking effect, well known to men everywhere, on his nether regions.

Four herders told us their reindeer were dozy and had little energy. Upon examination I saw none of the signs associated with the anaplasmosis I knew so well from the hundreds of cases I'd seen in my Kenya days. There it was associated with anemia that led to pale membranes of the eye, the tongue and inside of the mouth. Constipation was always a symptom. The temperature was usually higher than normal. But here the only sign was lethargy. The herders reported that their animals didn't go far from camp to eat. After conversations with Nansalmaa, it seemed likely that we were indeed seeing the anaplasmosis that was confirmed by our DNA work in Saskatoon.

Now that we had that diagnosis I could proceed with the treatment that worked so well those 35 years ago and is reported to still be effective. Ganbat explained to the owners that it would take a while for the patients to regain their vigour. Time would tell.

We left the camp in the early morning and started to climb. The narrow track, only one horse wide, wound up between the trees. As on previous trips, the men chanted a long traditional Mongolian song that sounded like a dirge to my untutoured ears. After they'd finished, I let rip with the campfire song, "Green Grow the Rashes Ho" that I'd learned as a Boy Scout.

The climb went on relentlessly. Three hours later my horse suddenly jumped up a big step over a rock. Perhaps I had dozed off or was not paying attention. My sternum met the metal ring at the front of the saddle in an altogether too violent collision. It felt as if I'd been sucker-punched by Muhammad Ali.

Once more above the treeline, we stopped at a camp with only two urts and a few reindeer. I was feeling sore, very sore. My ribs ached and I wondered about a bruised liver. The blue tent Morgan had brought along beckoned. I took a couple of painkillers, opened up my sleeping bag and lay down. The team took off for a nearby camp to do some more sampling.

Sometime later I woke from a doze and heard the clicking of reindeer feet and a scraping sound. A peek out of the tent flap revealed why. Two reindeer, led by man with a dark del and a white hat, were harnessed to poles they were dragging through some scrubby brush. He untied the ropes next to the fire pit and the deer wandered off.

Next morning the team headed back down to the camp where the *Ashes and Snow* crew were movie making. They'd gone. There were no urts there, just bare poles standing like pyramids, ready for the next visit by the nomads.

Several deer and some horses stood around, loaded with all manner of things. The families were in the process of moving to a new site. The khaki-coloured urts donated by the *Ashes and Snow* organization were folded and roped to the packsaddles. There were stoves, bedding, milk churns and who knows what else. Small children snuggled among and on top of all the goods and chattels of home.

There were only a few reindeer still tethered to logs. These had been kept back from the main herd to be checked after treatment. They had already started to recover, which was good news for their owners and for us.

It boded well for the future use of the correct drug for treatment of anaplasmosis cases by Borkhuu and Ganbat as they carried out their routine duties across both taiga regions. Second treatments were done by late morning. I showed the two guys the right doses for adult and younger deer by drawing up the clear golden fluid into syringes. After a snack we rode steadily for three hours.

When we arrived too early near the pickup point for our trip back to the village, Bayanmunk stopped and unloaded the horses. We sat and enjoyed a cuppa. I should have realized that the guys would certainly have the wherewithal and a supply of tea in their bags. The metal bowl emerged. A fire started and the water was soon boiling. The lack of milk was of no concern.

By the time we arrived at Tsagaan Nuur, the tense moments during the trip between me and Morgan had escalated. We agreed that I would not continue to the east taiga.

Gala drove me back to Murun, avoiding any glue-like swampy areas. In one of those karma moments, I was lucky enough to meet a woman who spoke fluent English and helped me negotiate the challenge of booking a ticket to the capital. There was no need to spend the night in this outpost town.

CHAPTER 21

Farewell to Mongolia

Back in Ulaanbaatar I checked into a hotel, caught up with Gana and left my del with her to pass on to Morgan in case any new volunteer needed one. I toyed with the idea of taking it home, but the temptation was trumped by common sense. I wouldn't be riding any horses in the near future.

An important task was to connect with a young woman named Khosbayar. I'd met her parents during that last trip to the nomad camps. Her father Byindalai and mother Tsetsgee from the west taiga told me that she would start her first year in vet school. Given that she was from the reindeer culture, I wanted to arrange some support to cover her tuition fee. It was modest, just over $300. Gana soon found her and during a lunch break the three of us headed to a local bank branch. It took a while to explain to the clerk what I had in mind, but ultimately we made the arrangement that Khosbayar would get my support for a year. Further support for the next three years would depend upon her transcript and a letter from the college showing she'd been admitted to subsequent years.

She spoke no English but would be taking classes. I gave her my email address and told her to email me in a year with her own letter.

During a break at Chez Bernard, I chatted with a couple of expats on short-term contracts to find out about possible tours with a local company. There were only a few days left and fishing was the first priority, a visit to the Gobi to follow. It turned out that there was exactly what I wanted a couple of blocks up Peace Avenue and just around the corner.

A short walk and there it was: Tseren Tours. At the desk stood Tserendolgor next to her Caucasian husband, who was holding a small baby in his arms. When he spoke, I at once recognized the Dutch accent and we chatted about that and my Dutch in-laws for a while. Tserendolgor herself arranged for a translator and driver to be at the hotel at 9:00 a.m. next morning.

A "Jeep" exactly like the UAZ I rode from Murun to Tsagaan Nuur on my first visit, the one I had to leave in haste every half-hour or so to deal with the epic aftermath of the tsoivan meal, picked me up at the hotel door.

"Are you Mr. Jerry?" asked the long dark-haired young woman dressed in a purple sweater and jeans. She introduced herself. "I'm Ankha, this is our driver, Ulzii."

I remembered that I'd heard his name before when Binde, our first-year translator, told me that the word means an endless knot that brings good fortune or blessing and ensures strength and long life. What a great name to give a boy!

"Sain baina uu?" he said. He was solidly built, slightly over-weight, round-faced.

Ankha checked that the most important thing was the fishing and we headed out of the city. The front passenger seat was no more comfortable than its 2004 relative. My knees still jammed against the dashboard. How Ulzii managed to drive, given that we are about the same height, remains a mystery.

The trip, on a narrow, tarred road, lasted for five-and-a-bit hours through a landscape of rolling hills turned brown in the autumn dry. After a brief conversation between them, Ulzii turned into a small town and Ankha entered a store. Ten minutes later she emerged with two plastic bags and explained that she'd picked up some supplies for our meals. We carried on for another hour.

I woke from a doze as we crossed a concrete bridge that spanned a 30-metre, fast-flowing river and at once turned onto a dirt track. We soon stopped beside a ger, an old red and white tractor parked nearby. Scattered cow pats around indicated that cattle were the livestock here. A man came over to chat. He pointed upstream and off we went, avoiding the deepest of the ruts. After no more than two kilometres, we crested a rise and there in front of us were two more gers.

We all climbed out of the vehicle for a stretch. Ankha spoke briefly to a woman dressed in a royal blue shirt and purple trousers, her dark hair parted in the middle. She pointed towards the river. As we bumped over the rough ground, Ankha explained that the woman's husband was tending his sheep and also fishing.

Over a rise, away to our left, a flock of some 50 sheep, heads down, grazed on sparse grass. We heard a two-toned call from in front. Another small bank and there, in the middle of the river, stood a grizzled man in a gray coat, the brim of his battered hat turned up in front.

Two things identified him as a dedicated fisherman. First, a long rod held out to one side. Second, his hip waders tied to mid-thighs with some yellow cloth. He was concentrating on the water and barely gave us a glance. It was obvious his sheep took a distant second place to his current activity.

Ankha introduced me and told me his name was Chalghasuren but he preferred Suren. She helped me ask if I might fish and also what he was using as bait. He pulled a small tin from his pocket to show several grasshoppers. In turn I opened a small tin of little streamer flies, muddler minnows that I'd tied back home. They have served well as wet flies in the past. He shook his head, said something and made a little *mm-mm* grunt. Ankha translated the obvious message: "He thinks there is no chance."

I set up my fly rod, chose a reel with a pink floating line ending in a three-metre brown sinking tip, attached a muddler to the tippet and moved 100 metres downstream. A cast across the flow, letting the line curve gently down, at first produced no results.

After letting out a metre or so off the reel, with each cast the rod tip bent and at once came a surge of the adrenaline known to every rod and reel fishing fanatic. Soon a pan-sized, trout-like fish lay on the bank. It resembled the ones from Tsagaan Nuur — lenok. Four more followed in half an hour. Suren, who had six on the bank, grinned. He called the fish *zeveg*, which Ulzii explained was the local name for lenok. His heavy four-metre rod and spinning reel with no handle must have been given to him by a previous visitor. The outfit obviously worked for him.

Suren climbed up the bank and we headed back to the tent. Ankha introduced me to his wife Bayarmaa, who had directed us to the river.

Naturally, tea was soon passed round. I opened the tin of flies, passed it over to Suren and Ankha told him I'd tied them myself. At once the ice broke.

He grinned and we established some common ground. At 64, Suren was a year younger than me. I was brought up to never ask a woman's age, or her real hair colour, but Bayarmaa at once chimed in to say she was only 52. They had nine children. She was obviously proud to tell us that their youngest daughter, aged 19, was studying English and Japanese at university in the capital. I reacted with a nod, "Hmmm," and "good."

It was time for bed. Ulzii set up a small blue tent a short distance away from the ger. With sleeping bag in hand, I crawled in. A sheepskin mattress on the ground was a real delight. I'm not sure how long I stayed awake.

I'm an early riser. I stood to rub the sleepy dust from my eyes as usual and was astonished to see Ulzii out cold inside the Jeep, his head against the window. How a big man could find a comfortable position to doze, never mind spend the night in the sardine-can-like cab is still beyond me. Ankha emerged from the ger bright as a button, stretched once, shook her hair and headed away. She came back a few minutes later, looked over at the Jeep and explained that, when he was out driving with tourists, Ulzii never slept anywhere else. Even out here, in the almost deserted steppes of Mongolia, where his vehicle was hardly likely to be stolen. Ah, well! Each to his own.

After a cup of tea with our hosts and a couple of slices of the bread we had picked up the previous day, we headed upstream in the Jeep. I wanted to explore the river to see if there were any likely looking pools where they opened up below small ripples that might hold a fish. We stopped every now and again, but the muddler tempted nothing, or, more likely, there were no hungry fish at home.

However, for the amateur birder in me there were nice moments. We saw several birds, some of which I could even identify. On the water there were swans, several species of duck and a merganser with well-grown young in line behind. A gray heron stood statue-like on a sandbank mid-river. There were a couple of eagles, and a smaller raptor that looked like some sort of buzzard. The biggest surprise occurred when a covey of a dozen gray partridge, known as the Hungarian partridge in North America, jumped up in front of the Jeep. I've seen them in England and Germany but had no idea that they ranged this far east. It was no surprise that there were pheasants, not just the ring-necked that has been imported to so many countries but males of two other species, equally gaudy but with different plumage. I knew that across Southeast Asia there are a variety of members of this family, but I had no idea which one these beauties were.

The evening's fishing back at the ger was just as productive as before. Between us Suren and I landed ten. Another excellent supper followed.

Next morning we headed out. Suren nodded in obvious delight when I gave him my little tin of muddlers. It meant he could continue to fish when the grasshoppers were no longer hopping as the autumn progressed and the temperature dropped.

From the pleasures of good fishing, we headed further south towards the Gobi Desert. There wasn't much time to explore this region. There was only a day and a night before I had to return to UB, spend the night in the hotel and catch the early flight to Beijing.

The landscape soon got drier, the grass sparser. There were almost no trees in sight. Rolling dunes were the main feature. We followed a windblown track that snaked across the sandy soil. Every now and again massive rock formations broke up the scene. Four uncomfortable hours later, we rounded the edge of another rocky outcrop and stopped at a thorny bush that seemed to emerge from a mass of strips of blue cloth.

The bush, standing four metres, was growing in isolation at the foot of the rocks in the middle of nowhere. The fissure behind must bring sufficient rainwater, when it does actually rain, to keep the plant alive.

An hour later we stopped at a single ger where three young men had some horses tied up. There was little vegetation around. I wondered how on earth the animals survived. The guys had no concern with protocol. Ankha and Ulzii entered to the right. We sat anywhere. Instead of tea, we were offered a foul-tasting milky drink. After my obligatory sip, I put it aside. Ankha did the same, while Ulzii had no trouble with his bowl. Ankha explained that this was fermented mare's milk, the airag Lil had warned me about when we first met. After Ankha told the men about me the conversation, or the bits of it translated, was entirely about horses. All, except Ulzii in his Jeep, crashed on the ground in the ger, although I did get another sheepskin mattress.

In the morning we headed back to the capital. One more night at the UB hotel and off to Beijing, the crazy crowded airport, another night and then an early flight across the Pacific and home.

Part Three

RESULTS AND
CONCLUSIONS OF
THE WORK IN
MONGOLIA

CHAPTER 22

The Artificial Insemination Issue

When Morgan came to Saskatoon in April 2004, she mentioned that one of the concerns the herders have was a lack of diversity in their herds. They had asked about the possibility of AI using semen of bulls from other places to reduce inbreeding. Other than AI, new blood could be brought in by the translocation of live bulls from similar but long since separated herding cultures.

Whether either or both are carried out, the first issue to be considered is the ancient culture of the people and their herds. The Tsaatan and their close neighbours in the Tuvan region of what is now Russia have bred their reindeer for specific characteristics for at least 3,000 years, maybe even the 5,000 that some have suggested. Before the border closed, the people shared culture and spoke the same language. Over those many years, the deer's characteristics that suited the people were that they would be so tame that they could be ridden, milked, harnessed and used for packing almost anything.

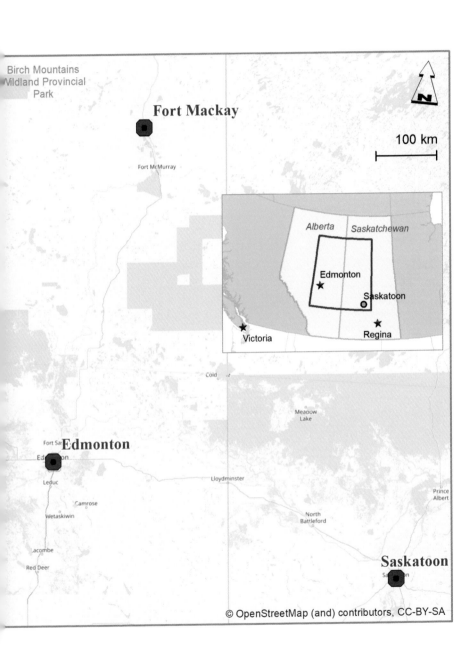

The Birch Mountains at top left, 800 (km) bird fly distance from Saskatoon.
(Provinces of Saskatchewan and Alberta inset).

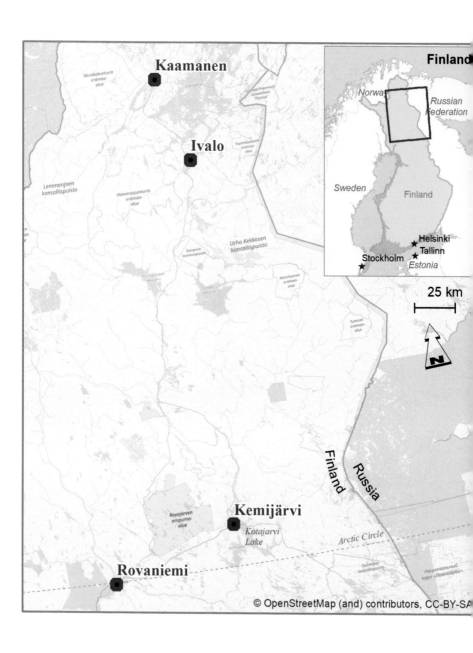

Part of the reindeer herding region north of Rovaniemi (Finland inset).

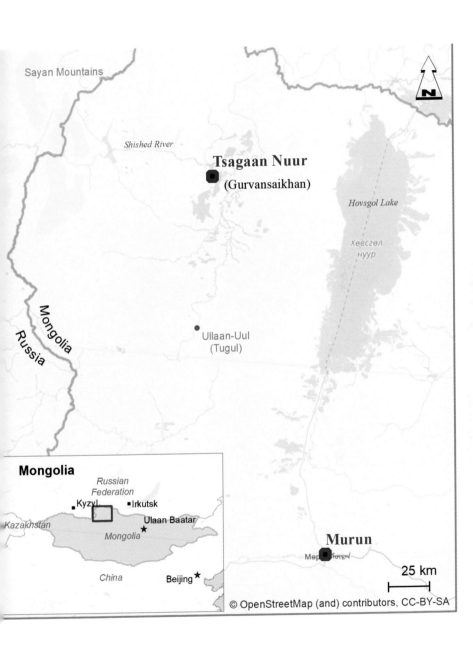

From Murun to Tsagaan Nuur and the Sayan Mountains (Mongolia inset).

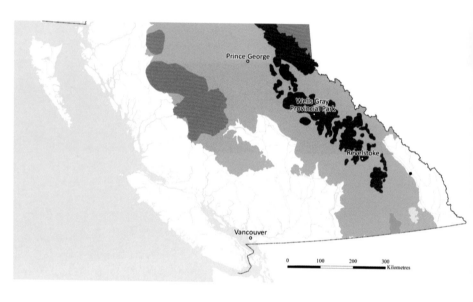

Map of southern British Columbia showing regions where caribou are currently present. Colour codes are as follows: Yellow: Historic Purcell South range. Blue: Historic South Selkirk range. Dark red: Current range of the southern group of Southern Mountain Caribou. Red: Historic range of the southern group of Southern Mountain Caribou. Grey: Current range of the northern group of Southern Mountain Caribou. Black dot: Proposed site for the SMC DU9 Conservation Centre. *Map Courtesy of Caribou Conservation Breeding Foundation.*

ABOVE FROM LEFT Elaine Wirtz out for a ride with Miss Mini Miracle and Raffi the dog, Wadena, SK. *Courtesy Charlene Wirtz*; Uganda kob male in Murchison Falls National Park, Uganda — an unlikely Rudolph. BELOW A Christmas parade in Scotland. *Courtesy Cairngorm Reindeer Herd.*

ABOVE Who is this guy? Let's check him out. *Courtesy Bill Coyle.*

BELOW Jerry Haigh and Bob Stewart bulldog a moose.

LEFT Flying elephant in Rwanda during a 1975 conservation program.

ABOVE After the antidote, a caribou bull is up and away.

BELOW When it's cold outside. Weighing a woodland caribou in northern Saskatchewan.

ABOVE FROM LEFT Reindeer on the road. *Courtesy Finnish Reindeer Herders' Association archives*; A bull among the trees. *Courtesy Anne Ollila.* BELOW Ruska autumn colours seen across the lake from Mauri Nieminan's home. *Courtesy Mauri Nieminan.*

ABOVE Jo in Santa's workshop. With the red and white coat, red and white hat and reindeer hide seat, is she auditioning for a role as Santa's helper? BELOW A group feeding on lichens and vascular plants during a summer in Finland. *Courtesy Tarja Konstig.*

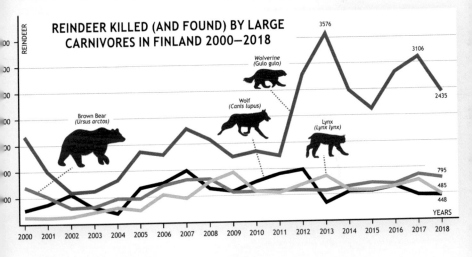

REINDEER KILLED (AND FOUND) BY LARGE CARNIVORES IN FINLAND 2000–2018

Wolverine
(Gulo gulo)

Wolf
(Canis lupus)

Brown Bear
(Ursus arctos)

Lynx
(Lynx lynx)

3576

3106

2435

795

485

448

YEARS

REINDEER

2000 2001 2002 2003 2004 2005 2006 2007 2008 2009 2010 2011 2012 2013 2014 2015 2016 2017 2018

THIS PAGE FROM TOP A female reindeer hitched to a nearby tree waiting for her owner to come and collect her; Known wolverine kills exceed, by three times, those by all other predators. *Courtesy Aarre Jortikka.*

FACING PAGE FROM TOP Mustering a herd in Finland across the treeless landscape with a single snowmobile. *Courtesy Jouko Kumpula*; Cut out from the main herd, a small group is brought into the handling pen. *Courtesy Finnish Reindeer Herders' Association archives*; A discussion in the corral.

ABOVE FROM LEFT A contortionist bends into a seemingly impossible position; a figure dressed as a shaman gyrates to the music. BELOW The lion statues at the gate of the Children's Garden.

ABOVE Shopping centre in Murun. BELOW Liliana Goldman Carrizo and Dad'suren playing a long song. *Courtesy Allan Coukell.*

ABOVE FROM LEFT A khainag (yak–cattle cross) gives us the once-over; Motorcycle breakdown. How long had they been waiting? BELOW Looking out to the horizon. What is she dreaming of?

ABOVE FROM LEFT The little girl in the bright blue del, holding her baby sister, grins as she looks at the photo I just took of her. *Courtesy Bill Coyle*; Doing the chores. With a little help from my friend, to misquote the Beatles. BELOW The ger with the beautiful door.

ABOVE FROM LEFT A traditional Mongolian saddle; A much-used Russian military saddle.   BELOW Three hats – Ganbat between me and Borkhuu. *Courtesy Meagan Flenniken.*

ABOVE FROM LEFT A tall ovoo festooned with blue cloths and carvings; The view. The urts are the tiny white triangles in the middle ground. BELOW Morgan eyeing a reindeer, or vice versa. *Courtesy Meagan Flenniken.*

ABOVE Mum and Dad with their small child on his totem reindeer. BELOW FROM LEFT Urts with a solar panel and a satellite dish. Now the family can watch TV; The kitchen area in the urts. Antlers make great hooks for hanging milk churns and Thermos flasks.

ABOVE Bolorama (left) and Narantuya mustering the herd in the evening.

BELOW FROM LEFT Ghosta cradles his toddler; Erdenchimeg at milking time.

A del and golden yellow boos – the perfect coat. *Courtesy Meagan Flenniken*

A boy and his imagination. A dragon, maybe?

ABOVE Ganbat on Khurlee's right. Borkhuu with another cigarette. BELOW Moving the family, bedding and goodness knows what on reindeer and horses (note the father's traditional hat).

ABOVE   Enjoying prints of last year's photos. Byamba nearest camera, Morgan, Punstal holding the photos, Tsend and Punsil (identity of standing person unknown).
BELOW   The Hovsgol Mountains across the lake. He's hanging out with his horse and she's filling water containers.

ABOVE A lone larch marks the top of the treeline.

BELOW Down we go. The horse knows where he's going. *Courtesy Bill Coyle.*

ABOVE Dawn in the valley. Icing sugar everywhere.

BELOW Soyan and her patient. *Courtesy Byamba*

Bayanmunk and his horse take a breather at the top of the pass.

Straight out of the mountainside at 2500 metres. Cold or what? Sore back solution!

ABOVE The dancers twirl in time to the music. Part of the greetings to the incoming vet students.

BELOW The rider, the horse and the fiddle. The statue at the entrance to the city of Darkhan.

ABOVE After our 22 hours stuck in the swamp, a three-ton truck comes to the rescue.

BELOW A cream and bread sandwich – perfect hedonism – food for the soul. *Courtesy Meagan Flenniken.*

Bill Coyle in a relaxed mood. *Courtesy Meagan Flenniken.*

ABOVE Suren the fisherman.

BELOW Five pan-sized lenok, a rod and reel and a muddler minnow.

ABOVE Ulzii, Suren, Bayarmaa and me enjoying a fish supper.   BELOW Reindeer reflections across the lake. Sanjim leads his animals along the shore.

There are herding cultures in Russia whose reindeer have almost the same characteristics. Professor Vitebsky witnessed all of these activities when living with the Eveny of Russia. He described how most selected for milking were caught with a lariat, pulled to logs and tied with ropes before the event. There are YouTube videos showing Russian herders using lariats with great skill to catch males and even the females on occasion. A lariat was never used during the many times I watched the reindeer coming back to camp. They are not needed. Bulls that need such a degree of control would not qualify as sires.

One thing that we did not see in Mongolia was the use of reindeer for pulling sleds. Russian military use them in this way. Considering the mountainous terrain in the taiga, such an attribute would have been quite useless.

As Dr. Tyler said, reindeer have no problem dealing with temperatures down to minus 30°C, but in the more northern herding cultures the animals have not needed to be selected to withstand summer temperatures of 40°C, as can occur in Mongolia, or have the white colour for which the Tsaatan have selected over the generations.

They occupy an important place in the people's spiritual lives. Such animals are given as sacred totems to children, as I learned during my first trip, when a little boy, less than a year old, was hoisted onto his deer and held by his parents.

In no other herding culture do the animals have the same set of attributes.

There is one complication. The herders repeated what they had told Morgan about the incestuous matings. These occasionally produced calves without hair or with deformed jaws. Even before the translation, it was easy to recognize the latter deformity when a woman used a hand and mouth gesture to pull up her top lip and push her lower jaw backwards, thus showing off her teeth. She was demonstrating what is known as parrot-mouth, when the upper jaw overshoots the lower by a considerable margin. Both are known results of inbreeding in sheep and other creatures. When the Tsaatan see such calves, they slaughter them at once, not for any ritual reason but because they will have little or no chance of surviving.

Another known result of inbreeding is the birth of females with abnormal udders, mainly missing teats. I saw three such individuals. One had only two teats, the others three. As I didn't see all the female deer on any of the trips, I have no idea if there were more than the three of these cows.

We couldn't get a total for the numbers of recorded inbreedings. There didn't seem to be any written records that would provide such data and Morgan suggested that one be started. I'm not sure if that happened.

A simple solution might be to arrange swaps of bulls between camps, or even across the river between the two taiga regions.

Despite the stories of those abnormal calves, and before proceeding with an attempt to bring in new genetic material by either bull importation or AI, the genetic makeup of the entire herd needs to be considered. Is importation really needed?

The results of work on the measure of genetic variation (heterozygosity) of the Tsaatan reindeer have been studied, as has the variation in many other domestic herds further north.

The first report about the genetics came in 2003 when Kirk Olson and his colleagues collected samples and studied the issue among 147 animals in the west taiga. Their results do not support the idea of inbreeding as a threat to the population.

In 2005 and 2006, when Vicki Gerwing joined our team to extract the DNA, we sent 92 further samples collected from both taiga regions to Dr. Røed at the Norwegian School of Veterinary Science. His results were similar. Dr. Røed has expanded his work to cover many more herds. In 2018, when I asked if he had any new figures, he wrote,

We have up to now analyzed about 30 different herds (more than 500 reindeer) of wild and domestic reindeer across Russia…The Tsaatan reindeer reveal a genetic pattern very different from all other herds. The amount of genetic variation among the Tsaatan reindeer are somewhat lower than what we see in most Russian herds, but to my mind not dangerous low. They reflect a population of reindeer which have been isolated from other reindeer populations for a very long time.

He also wrote, "There are several reindeer populations out there with lower variation that appear to do fairly well."

If new blood (genetic material) goes ahead anyway, despite these results, the simplest means that requires none of the detailed laboratory work needed for AI programs would be to transport bulls by air. The shipment would have to take place in winter when the antlers have been shed, the testosterone-driven aggression has abated and the ambient temperatures are cold. It would also be important to ensure that the food types from source are the same as at destination.

Whichever way new genetic strains come in — frozen semen or live animals — the bulls must come from herds as near as possible domesticated as those of the Mongolian ones. Others, like ones from Scandinavia that are not ridden, would not be suitable. If for some reason bulls cannot be obtained, the other possibility in which the Tsaatan expressed interest was the use of AI. Morgan told me that the literacy rate among the Tsaatan is over 95 per cent. They are well aware of the possibility of its use.

Getting semen to the taiga and its successful employment requires careful attention to two components. The easiest element is the collection, freezing and transport of the semen, which has been successfully carried out to a limited degree in reindeer. It has been done with many other species, including horses, sheep, and dogs, as well as millions of cattle for over 90 years. The first records of collection and successful use of AI in humans are known from the late 18th century.

I, as well as several others, have carried out this work with five other deer species or subspecies: wapiti/red deer, axis (aka chital), white-tailed and fallow deer. The semen is diluted (extended) and drawn into straws containing sufficient numbers of sperm to fertilize the eggs of each female. Up to 100 doses have been obtained from a single ejaculate.

For the Mongolian reindeer, semen would have to be collected from several males and used over a few seasons. There is no point in bringing it just from one or two potential sires. A one-off wouldn't be sufficient to seriously alter the makeup of the Mongolian herd. More animals with different genetic makeup would be needed in subsequent years.

The straws must then be transported in heavy insulated tanks full of liquid nitrogen at minus 196ºC right to Tsagaan Nuur. There they must be transferred to a so-called dry tank suitable for pack horse transport. Such tanks only hold the cold temperatures for 10–14 days. That would mean the need for nitrogen top-ups. That, in turn, would require a supply of liquid nitrogen to be available in the village. Possible, but not an easy option.

Semen collection and transport is the easiest part of the equation. Just a doddle compared to the work on the female side. Artificial insemination over widely spread camps in the Sayan Mountains would present a cat's cradle of complications.

The cows can only conceive if they are in heat. That happens a few times in fall and early winter every 18 to 29 days, on average 24, and may vary from cow to cow. It would be futile to simply show up at each camp and expect a cow or two to be ready on the right day.

The cycle has to be controlled so that cows chosen for the program are ready to be bred when the semen arrives on site. Such synchronization involves the use of hormones at specific times and then insemination at pre-set hours.

Knowing the time taken for travel between camps would be a basic requirement. In some cases distances might involve a short trip of only three hours, others as much as six, which would mean an overnight stay at one point followed by an early departure. As I know from my own experience with other deer, correct timing is essential.

For the actual insemination each straw must be carefully thawed just before use. On top of all that, the raw power of nature and sex drive has to be dealt with. A synchronized female will come into heat. It's not just the humans who will be interested in her. There are bulls in every herd. As I told the folks at the gathering in Colorado, these bulls change from docile grazing creatures to raging sex maniacs in a few days. AI candidates must somehow be kept away from them.

Wild bulls that also live in the region are certain to be enticed by the pheromones wafting downwind. "Come on big fella, I'm waiting for you," is the hormonal message. The reverse is true. His wind-borne message would be a come-on for the cows.

It's widely acknowledged anywhere from Alaska across Eurasia that domesticated females are sometimes bred by wild males. The herders told me that when this happens the "cross-bred" offspring are too difficult to handle and aren't tame enough and are too wild to fit into the herd.

Some might think that if all the cows to be inseminated were gathered in one place the timing could be adjusted to suit. The owners would have to leave their camps with a few animals, trek considerable distances and hold the new "herd" together for a month. If cows of different groups were brought together, it's certain that competition among them to establish who is the alpha would take place. The stress due to the departure from familiar herd mates, the appearance of new ones, the alpha disputes and a new human herder for some cows could easily disrupt the hormone program.

The other element for either import is the little matter of permits. Not so little. It's probably the toughest of all the hurdles to clear. Permit permission also involves politics. If a decision were made to proceed, the simplest method, one hopes, would be the shipment of a few bulls from Russia. The airstrip at Murun is a possible destination.

Getting permits for the transport of semen, frozen in liquid nitrogen, across international borders can be a very slow process. The caution is justified. In this case there would be a disease question about the originating herds. Thorough testing would be needed. The same with the extenders. The best extenders contain egg material. Is that a risk? The eggs have to be certified disease-free. However, it's not impossible. It is routine for many species. I jumped that hurdle with wapiti semen to New Zealand in 1980.

A conclusion? Is artificial insemination or bull importation to be or not to be? That is the question. Considering the genetic status of the Mongolian deer, the cost, the technical challenges, the permits needed and the political concerns, probably not.

CHAPTER 23

Disease Studies

As well as the inbreeding situation about which the herders were concerned, diseases were a key matter.

As I wrote in Chapter 17, Nansalmaa had been suspicious about the bacterial condition anaplasmosis for some time. Our DNA studies in Saskatoon confirmed her observations. It was a surprise to learn that Dr. Hill identified the sheep type (*A. ovis*) as the culprit.

There are a few species of the bacterium that affect different species of mammal. These include humans, dogs, cats, horses, sheep and cattle. It's the cattle one with which I am all too familiar. I must have seen hundreds of cases in the ten years I worked in Kenya. It's not contagious but is usually spread by blood-sucking ticks.

Under the microscope the bacteria appear as dark spots seen inside the red blood cells. When they reproduce, the cells rupture and the animal may become anemic. There have even been cases of sudden death. One thing we didn't see in the reindeer, but is normal in cattle, is constipation.

The intriguing thing is the way it turned up in an astonishing 80 per cent of our samples. In the fall, when we made our trips to the taiga, the tick season was over. However, in June 2007, when ticks are active, Dr. Sophia Papageorgiou detected a high prevalence of tick-borne pathogens in livestock, particularly in the reindeer in Hovsgol aimag where we worked. As well as the evidence of *A. ovis* that we detected, she found two others.

Happily, the condition can be treated and the drug we took in 2006 is the one of choice. The bigger issue will be how to ensure that Ganbat and Borkhuu are supplied with the drug for use in following years when it's needed.

The other major disease is brucellosis. It may be more serious than anaplasmosis because there's no treatment for animals, although thankfully there is a protocol for humans involving at least a six-week course of antibiotic.

Our card tests showed that 17 per cent of the Tsaatan reindeer were infected. In 2003, the year before my first trip, wildlife biologist Kirk Olson and anthropologist Hamid Sardar-Afkhami's results were 16 per cent positives. The slight difference is trivial. They closely match those of Dr. Erdenebaatar in whose lab at the veterinary school in UB Vicki Gerwing was able to extract DNA to send to Canada.

There is a critical point. The card test we used is ideal as a field test because it's easy to transport. However, given the conditions under which we, as well as Olson and Sardar-Afkhami, had to work, it needed to be confirmed with other tests in a controllable laboratory setting.

We ran three such tests in UB where wind and temperature were not factors. Two of them came up with positive results. Dr. Erdenebaatar ran two different tests on different reindeer because, according to the local veterinary services, there was a likelihood of brucellosis being present. The first was similar to, but slightly different than, our field card tests.

His first test result revealed that 15 per cent were positive. He then ran a second, different, test that came up with the same answer and confirmed his results.

It was Ian Fleming, in his *Goldfinger* James Bond story, who wrote: "Once is happenstance, twice is coincidence, three times is enemy action." Given that thought, which I have found applies to many situations, it's almost certain the disease is present in the herd. In this case four tests, not just Bond's three, showed positives.

In the context of the Mongolian and some Russian reindeer, as well as caribou in North America, brucellosis can be a serious problem, which is bad enough. In the first two years of the study, we saw 22 deer with swollen joints. That's 22 of 147, 15 per cent of the ones we examined. Way beyond chance or even traumatic events. There may have been others we didn't see. Swollen joints are a feature of this disease in many species. The most dramatic I have seen were in Cape buffalo in Uganda. One swelling was three times the size of a grapefruit.

The critical subject in dealing with this nasty disease is the question of control or eradication. There are three possible options.

One choice has been vaccination. Specific vaccines have been developed for cattle, as well as one for goats and sheep. Dr. Bob Dieterich and Jamie Morton tested several of those established vaccines in Alaskan reindeer. The common cattle one, known as Strain 19, caused an active infection in test reindeer. One of the vaccines that Dieterich and Morton developed proved to be highly effective. It maintained full protection against a challenge with the natural reindeer organism for two years.

A second method, test and slaughter, has often failed. There are at least two reasons. One is the matter of false negative tests that can occur, although Dr. Dieterich told me that when he used the Brewer card test for Alaskan reindeer destined for the lower

48 states none of those that came up negative showed subsequent signs of the disease.

The other reason for this failure is that the bacteria can persist in the environment. If all positive animals are removed from the herd, others that tested negative but were actually infected can still transmit it or can pick it up from the contaminated grazing spots where it has persisted, which it may do for months, especially in cool conditions. We worked at altitudes above 2000 metres, so cool is not unheard of.

The third response has been the eradication of entire herds where positive lab results were seen. In several countries, including Canada, the Unites States and the UK, it was the main tool and proved effective in dealing with the problem in cattle (although in both North American countries the disease is still present in wild herds of bison).

The results of eradication are recorded in Vitebsky's *Reindeer People*. In 1990 a positive test for brucellosis was made at one farm. As he wrote,

> In October 1990 the Old Man and his sons were forced to participate in what must have felt like carnage rather than harvest, and to join the Farm's vets with their own hands in wiping out their own glorious herd of 2,000 reindeer.

The family broke up and the working men ended up "hundreds of miles apart."

If all the few hundred reindeer of the Tsaatan were destroyed, that would mean the end of the culture. In 2002 Sanjim told Morgan, "If our reindeer die, we die. They are not just our living but our life."

Herd destruction is not an option.

Ultimately, there are only two choices. The first and best would be to use the vaccine developed by Dieterich and Morton that proved to be highly effective and maintained full protection against a challenge with the natural reindeer organism for two years. The program would have to be continued for several years, being used for all new calves and repeated every couple of years for all the animals. In this way the Tsaatan reindeer would eventually achieve a total clean bill of health. Getting an import permit would be a serious challenge. There's a problem. The Alaskan vaccine is not commercially available and a whole lot more would have to be made. Because of international restrictions, its production would likely have to be carried out in Mongolia, which would further complicate things.

The other option is to do nothing. The disease will wax and wane over time but will likely never go away.

CHAPTER 24

Predator Problems

Carnivores prey on both free-ranging domestic and wild reindeer/caribou almost anywhere they exist.

I soon witnessed an example of this at the zoo in Saskatoon where I first saw a caribou in 1975. Some evil SOB forced open the gate of the wolf pen and the seven wolves escaped during the night. When the keepers arrived next morning, some or all of the pack members had climbed in and out of a nearby pen, leaving the blood-covered bodies of two caribou. It wasn't a question of hunger. The wolves were well fed on a daily basis. They hadn't even opened the carcasses but were surely acting according to inborn instinct. The police were called in and shot the entire pack.

In Canada, when it comes to attempts to halt the decline of caribou populations across the country (more of that in Chapter 25), most wildlife managers have suggested that wolves are the main culprits. Wolf culls, by shooting from helicopters, has been the principal control attempt but has not materially halted the population declines.

The role of bears as reindeer predators is also known across most areas of the species. While there are some cases of kills of adult deer, the majority of successes are of calves in the first month of life. After that first month, the juveniles can run as fast as their mothers and outrun a bear. Few, if any, ungulates can develop that rapidly after birth. At full tilt, grizzly and black bears can reach speeds of 60 km/hour, but only in short bursts, which is plenty enough to take down the very young.

Bears have been shown to be responsible for at least half of early calf mortality on studied ranges on which mortality levels can reach 80 per cent in some years. One recent study of seven camera-collared brown bears in Alaska revealed an average kill rate of 16 moose and 14 caribou calves per bear per year.

Bob Stewart and his team, with whom I worked on moose in the Saskatchewan River Delta in the late 1970s, carried out the only study that has been undertaken in Canada to determine the role of black bears as predators of ungulates. They actively culled 12 and 26 bears, respectively, from two separate treatment blocks (90 km^2 and 130 km^2) prior to the onset of the moose calving season. Subsequent surveys demonstrated a doubling of moose calf survival compared to control areas by early fall.

It's pretty clear that bears have a major role in those critical first few months of a calf's life, be it a moose or a caribou.

When it comes to domesticated reindeer that range over large areas, there are important differences between them and their truly wild cousins. Compared to wild caribou, a degree of the hardiness in domestic reindeer has been lost. Dr. Finstad pointed out that reindeer lack three vital instincts. A crucial survival one is reaction to predators. If a bear, wolf or other predator bent on a feast approaches, caribou will take off when it is still a good way away. Reindeer allow a much closer approach, which is not good for their well-being. As Finstad put it to me, "Reindeer are couch potatoes, caribou are marathoners."

One more important fact about the differences between the two is their behaviour as the time for spring calving approaches. There are two very different strategies employed by caribou at this time. There are herds that migrate year-round, and there are ones that live in the boreal forests.

The migratory caribou have traditional calving grounds and go there en masse to deliver. In what is known as synchronous calving, a great number of calves arrive within a few days. Wolves and bears know exactly where their meals are coming from at this time of year but cannot deal with all the youngsters, or indeed their mothers. Most calves survive because they grow up quickly and can outrun their pursuers by the time they are about a month old.

The most famous animals that employ exactly the same technique are the wildebeest of the Serengeti and Masai Mara in East Africa. Many calves are eaten, but many more survive. In their case the predators are, of course, lions and hyenas. The lions and hyenas follow the herds, trying to pick off any stragglers.

Domestic reindeer no longer have this instinct and may calve over a longer period. Therefore, with what is more or less an invitation to either a mid-morning snack (a newborn calf) for a few wolves, or a banquet of an adult cow with a starter of tender calf, wolves and bears can take their picks on a daily basis.

On the other hand, the cows of nonmigratory, forest-dwelling caribou in Canada and reindeer in Russia space out to calve, a wolf avoidance strategy that doesn't escape foraging bears, especially given their sense of smell, considered to be keenest of any mammal.

In some areas, wolverines have been shown to be the major predator of newborn calves. These predators are also known to kill adults. Dr. Helen Schwantje, British Columbia's wildlife veterinarian with the Wildlife Management unit of the Ministry of Forests, Lands and Natural Resource Operations, told me of a remarkable case when GPS radio collars revealed an extraordinary story. A collared wolverine killed a collared caribou in the northern part of the province. When wildlife officers arrived to check the lack of movement of the signals from the caribou, the tracks in the snow showed that the predator, rather than chowing down on a few meals, was enjoying a rent-free, full board-and-lodging stay. It had not only killed the big bull but had been living inside the carcass.

A study of wolverine predation in Alaska revealed that in one case a wolverine chased a caribou for 62 kilometres before killing it. Twenty kilometres more than the distance human marathoners cover! Long distance indeed, not for a gold medal but for a meal.

Other known predators of wild caribou are lynx and, of course, humans, both by legal and illegal hunting. Even golden eagles are known to sometimes take newborn calves.

In Finland, where long-term studies of predation have been conducted, compelling details of domestic reindeer predation have been collected. Wolverines, wolves, lynx and brown bears are the main culprits. Just as in the wild caribou of North America, golden eagles are also involved as killers of calves.

The Finnish Reindeer Herders' Association publication, *Damages Caused by Carnivores*, contains a graph that shows a steady upward trend of confirmed carnivore kills since 1987. Over 30 years they increased from under 1,000 to over 5,000 in 2017.

The authors make two important points: "The damage caused by large carnivores is a natural part of the reindeer husbandry," and "only about one-fifth of killed reindeer are ever found." It is thought that the actual number of kills lies between 25,000 and 35,000.

Some of the difference in the figures is certainly due to the fact that, in late spring, bears kill newborn calves (over 700 in 2,000), just as they do to the wild cousins. At that time, the animals have emerged from hibernation, have low energy reserves and are hungry. Evidence of such kills would be hard to find.

In the 13 years leading up to 2000, the data show that lynx were the main culprits, with bears a close second. Estimates in 1987 had it that either species made less than 200 kills a year. Lynx have spread all the way to the northernmost parts of the reindeer husbandry area. Previously, it was unknown up north, but it has become rapidly more common. In 2000 lynx killed over 1,600 head. In contrast to the findings of wolverine predation on newborn calves in Canada, these creatures, which have been protected in Finland since 1982, have become the main problem year-round.

In 2019 Anne Ollila wrote this to me: "Nowadays, wolverine is the biggest reason of the found kills, killing more than the other three (lynx, bear, wolf) together in winter." More and more wolverines have come over the border from Russia. They are members of the weasel family. The smallest male weasels weigh around 260 grams. Large wolverines can weigh a hundred times as much, up to 25 kilograms, although huge ones may weigh as much as 32 kilograms. Weasels have been known to massacre all the birds in a henhouse in a blood-soaked frenzy, euphemistically known as "surplus killing." In a similar fashion, a wolverine may kill several reindeer in quick succession. There are examples of a wolverine driving a black bear off a carcass. They are furred chainsaws.

In a YouTube video, ViviAnn Klemensson explains that they are long-distance runners that jump on a deer's back and sever the neck tendons. The victim can no longer hold its head up and staggers until it falls. The wolverine may then kill the reindeer at once, or simply torment it until it dies. A family of wolverines can get through 90-odd reindeer a year. They are so troublesome that for the last three winters eight hunting licences per year have been issued. Yet eight successful hunts to deal with kills of at least 3,500 head is like a dripping tap in a thunderstorm.

The Tsaatan herders consider wolves to be the major

predators of their precious animals. When I was in the taiga, I saw only one serious wolf-inflicted scar. It was on a reindeer's face. That one was lucky to escape.

Two-legged poachers are also involved. Not the odd poacher who takes an animal or two, or maybe even half a dozen, enough to feed a family or camp members. It is poaching on a big-money commercial scale. In northern Siberia's Taimyr Peninsula, huge numbers of the animals are killed at river crossings on their known migratory routes. In 2017 the slaughter was reported to supply the traditional Chinese medicine market, in which antlers are thought to be useful and even act as aphrodisiacs.

A September 2019 account tells of another mass slaughter across the region in which a single site covered six hectares. In this case the poachers took only the tongues! In both *Siberian Times* articles there are gruesome photos of amassed carcasses. The bodies were left to rot. These "surplus killings" that take place in a few minutes make bears and lynx, and even wolverines, look like lapdogs.

CHAPTER 25

Declines and Crashes of Caribou and Wild Reindeer

Four interwoven factors that lead to the changes in the numbers of wild members of the species across the north are well documented over time. In some cases the changes are dramatic and can be described as Crashes (with its capital C).

The dynamics are deterioration of the range because of overuse by the animals; encroachment by humans into their established ranges; excessive hunting; and changes in climate. Alone or combined, serious or catastrophic reductions of reindeer populations can lead to starvation for the people who have, for generations, relied upon them as food sources, shelter and clothing, which even includes the making of ropes and sinews for stitching.

According to the latest *Arctic Report Card* from the National Oceanic and Atmospheric Administration, the number of animals in all of the 22 herds monitored across Alaska's Western Arctic and across Canada from 1970 to 2017 has decreased to varying degrees. Five of them "have declined more than 90 percent and show no sign of recovery... Some herds have all-time record low populations since reliable record keeping began."

A 2018 article by Justina Ray in *Canadian Geographic* magazine reiterates Jim Rettie's statement that the major factor in declines is "industrial development, which fragments habitat." A detailed map that shows the precipitous decline of all herds in the country accompanies the article.

Striking examples in that article make the point. From a maximum number of two million, the barren ground caribou populations have collectively dropped to less than 800,000. The northern Quebec Leaf River herd declined by 92 per cent from 700,000 head in the early 2000s to 5,500 in 2018.

There is a single exception to these staggering figures. Extensive long-term research by scientists of the Porcupine Caribou Management Board shows that, from a population of 100,000 in 1970, the Porcupine herd of Northeastern Alaska and Northern Yukon has doubled in 50 years.

Declines in wild reindeer numbers are occurring across Russia. In 2018 Don Russell and his colleagues reported that the drops are especially apparent for three types of wild reindeer. Eighteen of 19 herds are decreasing, rare or threatened. In 2000 there were a million head in one herd. Nineteen years later, the estimated figure was only 400,000. The area is so vast that policing it is virtually impossible. Russian scientists take a pessimistic view and believe that the herd numbers will continue to decline.

Dr. Ivan Mizin of the Russian World Wildlife Fund has documented herd sizes of both wild and domestic animals. From a peak of five million in the 17th century, by 1900 wild numbers had crashed to 600,000. They halved again over the next 50 years and showed a slight increase to just shy of a million head in 2010. He concluded that the two main causes of the massive declines are habitat destruction and poaching.

In Alaska and Canada's Northwest Territories, there have been many natural fluctuations since scientific records were kept; the range between peaks and troughs is from 10 to 60 years. Indigenous histories reach back even further.

Accounts of thousands, tens or even hundreds of thousands of the deer returning to the same grounds over several seasons will steadily lead to degradation and loss of the lichens and vascular plants to such an extent that there is nothing left for the deer. The great herds of barren-ground animals that used to gather on the calving grounds, best known because of publicity, will no longer congregate.

The various subspecies of reindeer that occupy different parts of the north migrate to feeding areas according to what is available. The barren-ground ones may cover huge distances, moving to pastures where the most nutritious feed is available when it is needed for milk production and regaining body condition in preparation for breeding, followed by subsistence during the harsh conditions of winter.

It is also the season when bulls are growing their antlers, again in preparation for breeding, when the most impressive bulls will gain the greatest opportunity to pass their genes to the next generation. In summer, on the open tundra, the animals eat the leaves of willows, sedges, flowering tundra plants, small shrubs and mushrooms. In winter they move to areas where forests provide shelter and feed quality is much diminished.

Boreal subspecies don't move as far as their barren-ground cousins. Their travels mainly involve transfer from rich alpine pastures in summer to lower forested areas in winter, where they can shelter and find food, mainly lichens and some dried sedges and horsetail — the same plant used as "hay" for winter feeding of the domestic reindeer that I saw drying on racks in Finland.

In both kinds of habitat lichens are important dietary items that are consumed year-round. They are a complex mix of algae, bacteria and fungi that are slow growing and can take from 70 up to 230 years to regenerate. It is no wonder that repeated visits by huge numbers of reindeer will deplete the forage and cause loss of condition or starvation, especially of the calves that rely solely on milk for the first few weeks of life.

Dr. Nicholas Tyler, who, as I wrote in Chapter 2, has almost 40 years of experience with the smallest subspecies in the Svalbard archipelago, considers that the main component of the ebb and flow is normal. He wrote: "Wildlife populations are in a constant state of flux. There is no 'Balance of Nature'; rather, there is a perpetual 'Imbalance of Nature.' That is what gives Nature its dynamics."

One of the best-known examples of a so-called crash is the myth of lemmings rushing en masse over cliffs to their deaths. Maybe some folks even believe it. The myth dates back 400 years and was perpetuated by Disney's Academy Award-winning 1958 "documentary," *White Wilderness*. The suicide scene was created in the land-locked Canadian province of Alberta. The "sea" was the Bow River. Accounts differ; were they forced over a cliff, or were buckets full of the little rodents thrown down? The movie was even used in a 2008 US senate campaign ad.

In fact, lemmings are victims of their own success. They can breed virtually year-round. That's not all. They may be sexually mature within a month of birth, bear litters of as many as a dozen pups three weeks after mating and get pregnant while nursing young. It's a no-brainer to realize that such abundance must lead to a rapid drain on food sources and the death of thousands. Mass suicide over cliffs it is not.

When I asked Anne Ollila to comment about the dramatic rise and fall of lemming populations as it relates to Finland, she wrote to tell me about traditional knowledge that tells of the successive peaks of lemming populations always causing mass deaths of reindeer. It was assumed that the reindeer ate lemmings, and due to that they got sick and died.

Anne thinks the real reason for the changes is a combination of two facts. First, when

lemmings overgraze the pastures heavily, it affects not only lemmings but also reindeer sharing the habitats with them. Peaks of lemming numbers cause starvation of reindeer because the rodents devour the forage. Secondly, lemmings are an easy food source for all predators: wolverine, eagles, foxes, wolves, and lynx. When there are masses of these 'meatballs', as she calls them, are available, predator offspring have no trouble, and the numbers grow to their absolute maximum. When most of the lemmings die predators soon have no other food source left than reindeer. Both the peaks and troughs of lemming numbers mean losses of reindeer.

When reindeer diet resources declined or almost vanished, the animals either sought new grounds or died out — both are known.

Ernest Burch, in his landmark study of caribou in Northwest Alaska over a period of 15 years, wrote about the situation there. He recounted stories of several communities in which the disappearance of the caribou led to starvation and death of the people.

Another moving account comes from 1950, when Richard Harrington took an iconic photo of a starving Inuit mother pressing her nose and lips to those of her youngest child a few days before he wrote in his journal:

> Came upon the tiniest igloo yet. Outside lay a single, mangy dog, motionless, starving... Inside, a small woman in clumsy clothes, large hood, with baby. She sat in darkness, without heat. She speaks to me. I believe she said they were starving. We left some tea, matches, kerosene, biscuits. And went on.

Human Effects

All subspecies of reindeer are sensitive to human activities. The impact of human resource extraction and damage to habitat has been known for decades. Even when I worked in Saskatchewan and Alberta in the late 1970s and early '80s the population of woodland caribou was declining. As Jim Rettie, the biologist with whom I studied in my home province, later wrote,

> Reductions in caribou populations and their ranges are continuing as human activity erodes the margins of their distribution... The expansion of forestry, and of activities associated with oil and gas exploration and extraction, is further threatening caribou.

Beyond forestry and oil and gas exploration, there are several types of mining, all-weather roads, seismic lines, artificial light, noise, dust, airstrips, hydroelectric developments and pipelines. All have an impact. Tilly Smith, in *The Real Rudolph*, states, "Russia's track record during the Soviet years is appalling." She adds atmospheric nuclear explosions that released long-lasting radioactivity to the sorry list.

Wilderness tourism appears to have further compromised the herds. The destructive effects of all-terrain vehicles ploughing up the soil are but one part. In mountain areas, the popularity of heli-skiing steadily increases, the ear-splitting roar of snowmobiles criss-crossing the landscape and cross-country skiing at lower elevations all contribute.

The packed snow trails left by snowmobiles and cross-country skiers both flatten and harden the surface. They make life easier for caribou as they search for food. The wolves take full advantage of this, as they also don't have to struggle through soft and sometimes deep snow.

On top of that, roads and the many kilometres of seismic lines used for exploration of potential oil and gas sites, like those I saw stretching away to the horizon when working in the Birch Mountains of Alberta, have made life easy for predators. The cutting of trees and clearing of natural vegetation, followed by regrowth of young plants, has attracted other herbivores, especially moose and mule deer. The increased presence of these two species has attracted predators such as wolves that have an easy time running without the effort of having to sink into snow with each stride. Caribou using these "highways" (compacted travel corridors) then become a more frequent part of the wolf diet.

Added to these disturbances that have taken place over the last decades are the 2016 elections in the United States. Oil and gas exploration has increased. In December 2020 President Trump announced that drilling rights in the Arctic National Wildlife Refuge would be auctioned off on January 6, 2021. It is the largest national wildlife refuge in the United States and the calving ground for the 200,000 members of the Porcupine caribou herd that migrates hundreds of kilometres from the Brooks Range in Alaska to reach the area in spring and Yukon members of the herd. If the plan went ahead, the impact on caribou would be disastrous. One of the first actions taken by US President Joe Biden was to rescind his predecessor's order.

Hunting

Hunting is another human activity that in the last two centuries has gone beyond, in some cases way beyond, the basic needs for survival. While hunting is a basic life activity for northern people, excessive hunting has sometimes been a major factor affecting reindeer numbers. When American naturalist William Dall came down the Yukon River in the winter of 1866–1867, he wrote, "An enormous herd of rein deer [*sic*] passed so near Saint

Michaels that a 6-pounder loaded with buckshot was fired at them. Hundreds were killed for their skins alone." The following June he recorded that, in Anvik,

> The village was full of fresh skin of the reindeer fawn. I counted a thousand and seventy-two bunches hanging up to dry. Each bunch contained four skins, enough to make a parka. This would give a total of nearly four thousand three hundred of these little creatures, which had been killed during the last two months.

Another observer was artist-naturalist Henry Wood Elliott who, in 1875, reported about heavy trade in such skins at the communities of Nushagak and Ugashik on the south coast of Alaska. The coastal trading was a response to the demand for skins and meat by Europeans.

The arrival of rifles in the last three decades of the 19th century radically changed the efficiency of the killing. Bows and arrows, spearing, pit traps and chases are nowhere near as efficient. Ernest Burch referred to one record of the killing of 9,000 head in a few short months by members of one small community.

One example of local extinction comes from Alaska's Kenai Peninsula, where, in 1912, caribou disappeared, in part due to overhunting, although it's not clear if this hunting was for food or hides. It was only after reintroductions 50 and again 70 years later that they have become re-established, but the numbers are still small. The other cause was fire damage that, of course, affects habitat.

The people were no doubt killing to meet basic needs, but mass killings and trading have impacted caribou numbers, just as the recent mass poaching (for neither food nor hides) in Siberia, to which I referred in Chapter 24, has done.

Today, even in the acknowledged mass declines of herd numbers, hunting remains a vital part of Inuit life. In recognition of the crashes, several Indigenous communities across Canada have established controls on hunting that range from reduced harvesting to outright bans.

In February 2020 Eilís Quinn, writing for *Radio Canada International*, stated, "It's impacting everything from food security to culture to the transmission of the Indigenous culture from one generation to the next." She quoted Gregory Flowers, Nunatsiavut's Minister of Lands and Natural Resources, in her interview: "There's a lot more to caribou hunting than just harvesting animals. There's the preparation. There's talk and buzz in the community. The travelling 200–300 km, or even further sometimes to pitch your tent and do everything that goes along with caribou hunting. It's a cultural thing."

More recently, making access easier for hunters has become another cause of decline. It is only different in scale to the effects of commercial hardwood logging in tropical rainforests. Logging means heavy machinery and people. People need to eat. Bushmeat hunting (reindeer are a kind of bushmeat) is the natural result. Reports from 2001 and 2002 give estimates of up to some five million tonnes of bushmeat being consumed every year in the Congo basin alone. That involves as many as 587 million animals. Most of the meat is consumed in local towns and villages, but huge numbers are exported.

Climate

Climate conditions across the regions where the animals exist also have a marked effect on their populations. Indigenous accounts passed down through generations, reliable accounts from 19th- and early 20th-century naturalists and several science reports suggest that, with the one exception I describe below, the changes have a negative effect on reindeer numbers. The Arctic has warmed much faster than anywhere else on the planet. The changing ice conditions and glacier melting are well known.

These changes have impacted caribou distribution. In an interview with Heather Avery in March 2019, William Josie, the executive director of Yukon's Vuntut Gwitchin First Nation, suggests that, as weather patterns change throughout the territory, there is a corresponding shift in animals' traditional habitat. He thinks caribou are moving further north to escape the effects of climate change, specifically an increase in wet weather in spring that has had a direct effect on lichen growth, a vital part of the caribou diet. Instead of snow cover, through which the animals can dig with their forefeet, rainfall and freezing rain lead to ice coating the land, making it more difficult for the animals to reach the grazing.

Biologist Ronald Skoog noted that the most important time of year for caribou is the spring and early summer when those high-quality feedstuffs are essential. This is the time of year that females need the greatest food quality when heavily pregnant and for maximum milk production, vital for survival of the next generation. The warmer temperatures lead to earlier growth of plants and lichens. By the time the cows need the best nutrition, the value of the forage has started to wane.

There are short-term events — not to be confused with climate change — that can affect local reindeer numbers. For instance, in 1964, after a late winter thaw and a three-week delay in the migration to calving grounds, the loss of condition of the cows led to many deaths and poor calf survival.

Seventy years earlier, English naturalist Richard Lydekker described how, on the island of Spitsbergen, after animals faced snow-crusting conditions in spring, they returned to their coastal ranges "so poor as to be scarcely eatable." A more recent 2019 report by Sophie Lewis, again from Spitsbergen, tells of the death from starvation of 200 head.

Mining exploration and logging have a double-barrelled effect on boreal forest populations. For them an important component of their diet, especially in winter, is lichens hanging from tree branches, often called "old man's beard." In British Columbia, where reduced snow has been reported, caribou have been observed trying and failing to reach the "beards."

Higher temperatures also lead to the appearance of insects seen further north. In particular, mosquitoes hatching earlier emerge in their millions and survive longer, harassing the adults to such an extent that they spend less time feeding than is ideal and fail to gain the condition needed for successful breeding. The pests can kill calves outright.

While warming conditions have largely been negative, an interesting exception was reported in 2019. Dr. Mathilde Le Moullec of the Norwegian University of Science and Technology and her colleagues demonstrated that the overall Svalbard population has steadily increased over the last 100 years after hunting was strictly regulated in 1925. There are now some 22,000 animals on the island. Prior to that, since the 17th century, and particularly overhunting in the late 19th century, as human activity such as mining became established, hunting was a major factor that led to the disappearance of entire subpopulations.

She concluded that current and future population trajectories would likely be shaped by climate change. The temperature increases are already rising and will likely lead to even more food availability as the snow and ice disappear bit by bit every year and longer periods of greening of vegetation develop. This could result in greater carrying capacity of the land for the deer, in contrast to the negative effects of climate change reported elsewhere.

Fire

Fire, often caused by lightning, has long been a normal event in the north. It's a natural part of Arctic and boreal forest environment that occurs with differing frequency every year. However, changes in climate, particularly the fast-rising temperatures in the Arctic, have become another important component of the equation that has an impact on reindeer populations.

In the past it did do one important thing — it cleared the ground of old wood and brush, thus allowing new growth. Barren-ground caribou in Canada do not entirely avoid fire areas. They go near burn boundaries in older forested areas where newly regenerated forage is available to not only find lichens but also the herbaceous plants they favour.

However, the numbers and intensity of fires in recent years have increased to such an extent that alarms are sounding. Fires that have destroyed millions of hectares of forest where reindeer spend much of their time have turned the regions into food deserts. Some infernos burn uncontrollably for days on end. In many areas reindeer have virtually disappeared after large fires have ripped through the land.

Satellite photos of fires in Siberia show them raging in both forests and tundra. There are hundreds of them. In the latter the concern arises because the drying of the land due to rapid increments in temperature has led to so-called zombie fires. They are fires that seem to die down in winter, only to reignite in spring after remaining undetected in the carbon-rich peat of the huge swath of land that stretches right round the earth above the Arctic Circle.

Caribou of British Columbia

A well-documented example, with detailed information, describes the steady disappearance of caribou in the southern part of their range in western North America. In Canada's province of British Columbia, researcher Bruce McLellan made a thorough study of the long-term history of the southern mountain caribou (SMC) populations that once lived in the mountains of Montana, Idaho and southern BC (see the map of southern British Columbia in the photo section). From many written and reliable oral reports dating from the early 1800s, he describes the presence of the animals in the Bitterroot mountains of western Montana and southern Idaho to an area north of Prince George in central British Columbia, a distance of 1300 kilometres. Herd sizes varied from ten to several hundred.

To choose one of McLellan's examples among many is a challenge. Here is one. In what is now Wells Gray Provincial Park, 300 kilometres south of Prince George, great herds of caribou migrated across the valley each spring. Even in the 1920s, during the migration they were "impossible to count." It was in that area that the local names of Battle Mountain and Fight Lake are reminders of the wars fought between the Chilcotin and Shuswap for access to the bounty of the vital things in life.

McLellan noted that caribou are notoriously easy to kill once they have been found. In deep snow (more than two metres), when the animals cannot move at speed, many members of a single herd become easy targets. Just as in Alaska, repeating rifles replaced bows and made the killing faster and easier. Even Teddy Roosevelt (before he became president of the United States) got into the act, when he hunted them in southern BC in 1888.

By the late 20th century, when the use of helicopters allowed accurate counts, animals had disappeared in several areas. In others numbers were way down. McLellan wrote, "It is unlikely that the number of caribou before the 1980's will ever be known, but it is clear that in the late 1800's and early 1900's, they were far more abundant than they are today."

The status of the SMC population as of September 2019 was fragile (the northern one is endangered). The last one in Idaho was translocated to the Selkirk Mountains in British Columbia on January 14, 2019. That herd, one of the 15 small ones in the province, had 49 members in 2009. It now has none.

The grand total of all of the SMC herds in BC is no more than 1,200 head. Ministry officials estimate that 37 per cent of the deaths in two of the herds are due to wolf predation. Their population hovers on the brink, but efforts to reverse the decades-long drop in numbers are being made.

On a brighter note, in British Columbia there are community-driven initiatives to reverse the declines. They are teeter-totter endeavours, up down, down up.

My friend and colleague Dr. Helen Schwantje and her team in British Columbia are involved in a number of efforts with woodland caribou. In addition to assessing caribou herd health and building health and demographic baselines and trends, BC caribou workers are trying to protect, stop, or slow the declines of, and hopefully restore caribou across the province.

One method that has been used in attempts to save the scattered small groups is to move them into so-called maternity pens. This involves the holding of captured animals in a fenced area within the known range of the same subspecies. If the move is successful, the herd, now added to by the arrival of calves, is released into the local area.

The last South Selkirk cow and two cows and two bulls in the Purcell South herd were captured in 2018 and moved to an empty maternity pen at Revelstoke, where they joined an orphaned female calf from the last maternity penning episode. A cow from the local Columbia North herd was captured and all were held and fed together for over a month and released. They then joined the local herd successfully. This maternity pen is no longer in use.

One such project, so far successful, is located a thousand kilometres north of Revelstoke in the historical territory of the Klinse-Za People. It's a partnership effort between the provincial government and people of the West Moberly and Saulteau First Nations.

In 2013 there were only 38 head in the area, of which only 19 were cows. The population was steadily declining. In 2014 a penning program was started. Twelve to 18 females were brought to the pens each year in March before the calving season. They were then released in July, together with their now two-month-old youngsters.

After the pens were constructed, and wolf culling was started, the cow numbers have increased by about 7 per cent a year. In 2020 there were 90 animals in the group. Over that seven-year period, 60 calves have been released from the pens.

Another initiative to not only halt but to reverse the trend of the SMC herd's rapid slump is being conducted by the Caribou Conservation Breeding Program (CCBP). A nongovernmental organization called the Caribou Conservation Breeding Foundation (CCBF), of which one of the two founding members is veterinarian Dr. Amélie Mathieu, has been active in providing advice and support for the program. Dr. Schwantje is a team member.

The opening image on the CCBF's extensive website shows a single caribou overlaid with the words, "A Brighter Future for Caribou." Two relevant links are included. There is a proposed plan for the hoped-for recovery of the declining population.[4] The other is the detailed, 49-page, bilateral, February 2020 agreement between the BC provincial and federal governments.

The caribou account tells how caribou recovery through conservation breeding, by uniting caribou advocates and wildlife professionals, offers a hoped-for view of the future of the SMC. It recognizes the animals are classified as an endangered species

---

4   The plan, entitled *Recovery Strategy for the Woodland Caribou, Southern Mountain Population (Rangifer tarandus caribou) in Canada*, was developed in 2014 under the Species at Risk Act.

and states, "Conservation breeding does not replace other recovery measures and is different from maternity penning."

A conservation breeding program involves establishment of a dedicated centre where animals can be cared for on a long-term basis. Achieving this involves either gathering the animals from sites that have small numbers of captive members of a given species, or capturing small isolated herds from the wild and their subsequent movement to the centre.

The site also has fascinating and informative links. There are several references to programs involving conservation of species in other parts of the world. Among them are the stories of the takhi (the Mongolian wild horse) and the scimitar-horned oryx (a large North African antelope species).

The CCBP team is waiting for approval for a conservation centre plan submitted to the Caribou Program Board in 2019. They now wait for that approval and hope that a decision will be rendered by September 2020.

Dr. Mathieu wrote, "Other herds (Columbia South, Frisby-Boulder and Narrow Lake) are nonviable and will become extirpated regardless of actions taken on the landscape." The plan is to rescue those herds and bring them to the conservation centre site near Invermere, BC, which is the only suitable one CCBP has found. Its calves would one day be released as juveniles into extant viable herds to support their recovery.

Dr. Mathieu also wrote to say that if the timing had been different, the centre would have been built before any animals were brought in to form a founding stock for the breeding herd. But the three herds were already so small they couldn't risk waiting any longer. The hope is that the project will get approved in the next few months so that construction of the conservation centre can begin soon. A map of the region with the various fragmented herd sites is shown in the photo section.

Journalist Sarah Cox, writing in *The Narwhal* in December 2020, reported another more optimistic view of the hoped-for reversal of the caribou habitat in British Columbia. The provincial government has suspended, *for the time being,* plans to auction off cutblocks for logging 276 hectares of old-growth forest north of Revelstoke in the Selkirk Mountains. In the area there were 147 animals of southern woodland caribou hanging on. It was the largest remaining herd in the Kootenay region. The decision came after some 3,000 letters from scientists, conservation groups and the general public were sent to elected officials.

Disturbance that is bound to affect these caribou has already happened. Government contractors have constructed a five-kilometre road through the cedar and hemlock forest. It's not just the caribou. Populations of dozens of species of plants, animals and lichens will be altered.

"For the time being" is the double-edged sword. Cox quotes BC ministry spokesman Tyler Hooper about the suspensions, who said, in emailed responses to questions, that the government will "allow for further assessments about how harvesting activities might affect caribou in this area," and "this assessment is ongoing and no further timber harvest activities will occur in the area while the assessment is underway."

If the executives of BC Timber Sales (a government arm) decide that logging supersedes conservation, further roads will be punched in, the trees will be cut down and the landscape changed forever. The caribou herd will certainly suffer and likely disappear from the region, just as they have on so many parts of their former range where human impacts occurred.

As of March 2021, the approval of the CCBP program and the decision on the BC Timber Sales initiative have not yet been made. Both have consequences that will impact caribou survival in southern British Columbia.

Where Does All This Lead?

Given the declines and disappearance of the several things for which people use reindeer, as well as their cultural importance for Inuit and Siberians who rely upon them, the losses are major concerns. Other changes, such as the establishment of grocery stores in Canada, have reduced the reliance on caribou as a diet item, but not without cost. Groceries arrive by plane. The costs of air transport mean prices are three to five times higher than in Canada's southern cities. For instance, a four-litre container of milk costs around $20.00 in the north and only about $4.50 in Saskatoon. Other items such as snowmobiles, clothes, heating fuel and furniture come to coastal communities once a year by sea.

It was poet T.S. Eliot who, in 1923, wrote, "This is the way the world ends. Not with a bang, but a whimper." Across their entire range reindeer numbers are doing neither. It is more like a rolling thunder with an occasional tornado.

Some Indigenous People in North America believe that caribou will return. They likely will but only slowly. It will depend upon the regeneration of lichens, the principal part of their diet, that take many years to recover from the overuse by the animals, and the effects of fires. The consequences of the latter are just as serious as overgrazing. Studies have shown that lichen regrowth after burns can take anywhere from 10 to 500 years.

Until the lichens and the vascular plants upon which the reindeer also rely in spring and summer do return to the land, the animals will not come back in a meaningful way. Those natural increases will be negatively impacted by human-caused actions. The question about returns of these iconic creatures remains: How soon and how many?

CHAPTER 26

Domestic Reindeer
Ups and Downs

The ways in which human activity has affected wild reindeer are well documented. Domesticated ones are in the same boat, with an added factor. The development of wind farming in Norway is, of course, a responsible and far-reaching effort to develop eco-friendly energy sources. However, the increased number of them has a negative effect on reindeer.

Professor Nicholas Tyler and his colleagues quoted a recent Norwegian government White Paper, which stated, "Progressive and effectively irreversible loss of grazing land is recognized as the single greatest threat to reindeer husbandry in Norway today." In 1900 over 90 per cent of the country where reindeer herding occurs was free of interference from infrastructure. In 2019 that amount had been reduced by fully 70 per cent.

Studies by Dr. Anna Skarin of the Swedish University of Agricultural Sciences, Uppsala, demonstrate that "the continuous running of the wind turbines making a sound both day and night seemed to have disturbed the reindeer more than the sudden sounds and increased human activity during construction work." A recent news report provides a good (bad) example. Wind farms adversely affect the way of life of Sámi reindeer herders in Fenno-Scandinavia. In a *Guardian* report of January 2021, Weronika Strzyżyńska quotes Áslak Holmberg, the vice-chair of the Sámi Council, who stated, "Studies and indigenous knowledge show that reindeer don't go near wind turbines. These areas are lost from use to the herders."

It's not clear from her article how Holmberg defines "near," but lawsuits in which reindeer herders seek to defend grazing land against intrusion are common. Frequently, they win and are awarded compensation. But the windmills and power lines remain. The times, however, are changing. Usually, compensation has been in the order of 150,000 Canadian dollars, but in a recent case the figure was over $13 million. This award indicates that courts are taking the problem of avoidance seriously. It comes as no surprise to learn the decision has been appealed to the Supreme Court. Should the herders win again, developers will have to do some serious thinking.

On the other hand, in an exciting new move, a Swedish program is having a positive effect. Jon Henley, reporting in *The Guardian*, tells of a new initiative to build a dozen overpasses, called Renoducts, across roads and railways. The aim is to allow the animals to forage further afield to seek new feeding grounds without becoming involved in vehicle collisions, or, if large herds are being driven across the human-built routes, to avoid the need for traffic or trains to be halted.

In Canada's Banff National Park similar structures allow bears and other mammals to cross highways without encountering traffic. The wardens take the process a step further. At each end of the bridge are small barbed-wire fences that offer little of a barrier to the animals but catch tags of hair in their spikes. By taking advantage of this simple and ingenious detective method, they extract DNA that tells which animals use the overpasses and how often they cross.

On the northern slopes of Mount Kenya, on a road I used regularly, a similar initiative, using tunnels as opposed to overpasses, has meant that elephants moving up and down long-established routes were no longer a road hazard. The highly intelligent animals took little time to figure out the new situation.

In terms of herd numbers, there have been changes over time.

The status, as of 2020, of the domestic deer varied across continents and countries. The 2018 figure of 15,000–20,000 head in Alaska that Dr. Finstad told me of had, within 18 months, shrunk to only 8,000. The dramatic drop is partly due to the loss of government subsidies, as well as a lack of business experience. It is quite possible that the rest had merged with wild caribou.

Mike Jablonski, president of the USA Reindeer Owners and Breeders Association (ROBA), reports that there are between 1,500 and 3,000 reindeer owned by some 60 people in half of the lower 48 states, ranging from northern ones like Minnesota and Wisconsin, through New York where he operates, to Texas. Most use the animals in parades, or, before COVID-19, in supermarket parking lots. Mike cannot be more accurate about numbers because Christmas tree farmers own just a few head for publicity and are not members of ROBA.

In southern regions of Canada's provinces there were a few small herds. In 2018 the Alberta association had ten members who farmed 135 head. By January 2021 there were only three farms still operating and they owned less than 30 head. In Saskatchewan the ten owners in 2006 had declined to just three in 2020, one of which had but a single animal. The association ceased to function in 2016. In Ontario there were only six people owning reindeer in 2021, most having only two head mainly kept by Christmas tree businesses as a way of attracting customers.

For all three of the Scandinavian countries reindeer herding remains an important part of the culture. In Norway, between 2013 and 2018, an increase in the number of animals slaughtered for the meat market has led to a steady yearly decline in overall numbers. From 248,000 head there were 35,000 fewer animals. Once more, as with the wild herds across the globe, further human incursion is causing grave concern among the Sámi People. It is a conundrum, a conflict between the drive for green technology and an ancient culture. A year later BBC reporter James Cook put it this way:

> They are fighting plans to mine for copper, which is in demand to build electric vehicles and wind turbines. The Norwegian government has approved a new mine in the north, which it says is essential to help the world economy move beyond carbon. "This is life changing," says Nils Mathis Sara, a Sámi chief who has been herding reindeer since he was 14. "If this mine becomes a reality, that makes the chance of survival impossible — both economically and mentally. At my age we can manage, somehow. But the young, they're in a dark, dark time."

The changes in Sweden are less pronounced. Between 1995 and 2017, Swedish numbers of reindeer managed in the 51 herding districts fluctuated by only 4 per cent near the quarter of a million mark. However, just as with wild herds, people are dealing with industrialization of logging and the reduction in arboreal lichens as old-growth forests are being cut to meet the demand for timber.

In January 2020 a Swedish Supreme Court ruling led to a new threat, because from that date the Sámi have the right to say who can hunt and fish on their ancestral lands. That threat has sparked a series of revenge attacks involving a spate of killings of reindeer suspected to have been carried out by Swedish neighbours in retaliation. In one chilling interview with journalist Paul Rhys, a herder reported that he found his animals slaughtered in the woods. He went on to tell how a man drove up and said, "You don't come here with your reindeer or we'll shoot them. We've already shot seven or eight, and if I meet you alone in the forest I'll shoot you too."

Environmental impacts for the Finnish industry, due mainly to forestry, matches that of the wild caribou in North America. Logging has a marked impact because 75 per cent of the reindeer graze on pasture in the forest. In addition to this, by 2000 all old forest stands (more than 120 years old) had gone, so the important lichen on those trees is not available.

In Russia the number of domestic reindeer has declined steadily. Professor Vitebsky wrote of the drop: "Russia's population of domestic reindeer has plummeted from 2.2 million in 1990 to 1.1 million."

In 2010 Russian biologist Leonard Baskin, reporting similar declines, wrote that in the taiga areas reindeer husbandry has almost ceased. It has been impossible to get current accurate figures across the country's 11 time zones, but there is no doubt that in some regions the culture has vanished.

Dr. Laura Henry and her colleagues provide detail of one example in which the changes have occurred among the Nenet People who are known for their 1000-kilometre biannual treks north and south to summer and winter pastures. Traditionally, they used harnessed reindeer pulling sleds to move the herds. Nowadays, they use snowmobiles and ATVs. They have washing machines in their tents and have TVs and cell phones. Many have a house in one of the villages.

In winter the people live in the south, where shelter among the trees is available and lichens are the main food source for the animals. It's in summer that human industrial impact is greatest. The herders trek their animals to the Yamal Peninsula on the coast above the Arctic Circle where the abundance of green vegetation provides ideal grazing. However, the peninsula, about the size of France, also has the largest gas reserves anywhere on earth. Multiple pipelines, as many as eight in parallel, each developed by individual companies, prevent any animal access. Furthermore, roads and railway interfere with grazing and movement in the same way as they do elsewhere but to a greater extent. Not only have they disrupted the traditional migration routes and broken up pastures, they have also impinged upon traditional sacred areas.

An important part of the summer diet for the people is fish. Oil spills and other waste products have polluted rivers, which have also become shallow. There is no flooding, so no fish. The fish move down to places where the water is constant but not always accessible.

On the brighter side, many companies have taken a responsible approach to the needs of the people. Some have built both over- and underpasses for the animals, but they are seldom coordinated, which means that the deer have trouble moving to fresh pasture. Some companies have also made the effort to accommodate herder needs and have built cultural centres, schools, sports halls and slaughterhouses.

Another feature of the people's lives is the requirement that children attend boarding school. These various transformations have led to the younger generations moving away from herding to seek opportunities in other professions.

Several articles in the spring 2003 issue of *Cultural Survival Quarterly* describe the situation of reindeer-based cultures in regions of Siberia adjacent to the Mongolian border with Russia and the northeastern corner of China. Most of the communities in the region are Evenki or closely related to them. Among them are the Tofa, Tungu, Tozhu, Sayan, Soyot and Viliui. They were subjected to the Russian and Chinese policies of collectivization and many people lost the knowledge of reindeer herding, as well as their languages.

While the loss of ancient reindeer cultures has largely been due to central government suppression, disease and trading have also had a role. Some local and regional administrations are trying to resolve the problems faced by the herders.

In Mongolia's Hovsgol aimag there have been major changes. In the two years after I left, Dr. Bruce Smith volunteered to go to the taiga with Morgan. He told me that things got a bit tricky. In 2007 some soldiers riding motorcycles tried to arrest them for no apparent reason. After some conversation with the party, they left.

The situation further deteriorated in 2008. A four-wheel-drive vehicle manned by soldiers, accompanied by the mayor of Tsagaan Nuur, showed up. The Itgel team was accused of lacking permits. With a SAT phone, Morgan called the relevant government minister who dealt with the situation. In addition, the folks with whom they were travelling supported them.

Nonetheless, the herders permitted only a few selected animals to be tested. Dr. Smith thought the embargo might have occurred because herders feared test and slaughter as a way of controlling the brucella situation.

One of the projects that Morgan and her team started up was to develop a visitor centre in Tsagaan Nuur. The objectives, as stated on the Tsagaan Community and Visitors Center (TCVC) website, were to provide a "gateway" for visitors to engage respectively with the Tsaatan and obtain all they needed for their visits to the taiga. The goals included construction of a building, help with advancement of education and improvement of livelihoods of the nomads, and development of the various skills to provide everything from guides and cooks to services for visitors. Another intended goal was to establish a self-managed micro-credit system for the people.

In 2011 two students from the Western College of Veterinary Medicine, where I worked for 34 years, visited Mongolia. Hezy Anholt and Dayle Borchardt, after chatting with me, chose to go to Mongolia as representatives of a great program called Global Vets. An enthusiastic response for donations to the Itgel Foundation from their classmates meant they were able to donate $1,000.

In August 2017 Canadian landscape planning and tourism development consultant Ulysse Girard travelled to Tsagaan Nuur and went on to visit the families of both the east and west taiga. In two detailed reports to the Itgel Foundation, he assessed the status of the centre and the economic status of the people. The TCVC had become neglected and was more or less derelict. He noted 22 major deficits. Among them were many structural ones, overall filthy conditions, trash and even the unsavoury condition of the outhouse. There were five other lodgings available for tourists. The average price per night was US$6.00.

The situation in the taiga has undergone much more dramatic changes.

A single event had a major effect on the culture. In 2011 Tengis-Shishged National Park, which encompasses east and west taiga, was established. The taiga area where the Tsaatan live occupies only the most northerly 20 per cent of the park.

A specific level of protection was given to allow for ongoing Tsaatan activities. Herding is still allowed, but hunting is not. Hunting for moose and other large mammals has been an integral part of their lives since anyone knows. The wild animals, rather than the reindeer, supplied the meat component of the diet.

Fishing and chopping wood, the latter without a permit, are also forbidden, but registered nurse Sas Carey, who has visited the region almost every year since 2003, saw people fishing and wood being used for cooking in August 2019 and is unsure if these orders have been rescinded. This has inevitably led to an in-depth 2016 *Guardian* article by Marine Gauthier and Riccardo Pravettoni headlined, "'We have nothing but our reindeer': Conservation Threatens Ruination for Mongolia's Dukha."

The ban on hunting has further exacerbated an already serious situation. When Kirk Olson and Hamid Sardar-Afkhami travelled to the taiga in 2003, they learned that there was an ongoing problem with declines in numbers of several species that were once important sources of food. Larger species, including moose, red deer, Siberian roe deer, wild boar and musk deer, were all prized as a source of meat. For food, as well as the fur trade, wolves, bears and several small mammals were also hunted. Numbers of the mammals had declined to the point that Tsaatan People had to resort to eating their own animals.

Olson and Sardar-Afkhami wrote about a straightforward example of this dilemma when they joined hunters.

> While in the taiga traveling with Dukha hunters, supplies were exhausted, and we were surviving on fried flour and tea for three days until a female moose and calf (the first we saw) was sighted and taken for food. All members of the hunting party immediately offered respect to the spirit of the fallen cow, and later acknowledged they would have preferred to not shoot a female with calf in tow but there was no choice at that point, we were starving and would have had no other choice but to kill one of the pack reindeer at some point. Split amongst 5 households, it was said that this was enough meat to last approximately 3–4 weeks.

The hunting ban and the expulsion of herders who take their deer outside the traditional areas of the park to seek grazing, thus breaking Mongolian law, puts the very existence of culture in grave jeopardy.

In 2011 Rebecca Watters of the Wildlife Conservation Society, who had travelled among the Tsaatan on several occasions when studying wolverines, wrote, "A horde of missionaries showed up while I was there, and people were irritated by that. I also witnessed some pretty bad behavior by tourists, including just barging into houses, and dumping all kinds of trash up in the camps." Having learned from Morgan in 2004 about 60 missionaries who offered running shoes to any who converted, I wonder how many other such proselytizing efforts have been attempted.

The discovery of gold in the region led to another change. A *Bloomberg News* article of 2012 relates that

> Mongolia's illegal miners…have come from all over China to seek their fortunes in a landscape out of Jack London's *Call of the Wild*. Murder and banditry abound — and men walk around drunk in the middle of the day and hope that the warmth of the vodka will keep out the cold of the -50ºC nights. Tsaatan reindeer herders make journeys ferrying supplies to the Ninja camps for a profit.

In 2013 Watters and her students "ran into herds of domestic reindeer that had been penned up for the winter in remote valleys but were told that all of the people were down in Tsagaan Nuur for the winter."

There are two sharply contrasting views of the status of the Mongolian herds. In 2016 Sardar-Afkhami, who had spent years living among the Dukha and continues to follow their way of life, told CNN journalist Nila Sweeney that the culture is dying. She wrote of his thoughts that there were once around 200 families in the taiga.

> Nowadays, he thinks there are probably only 40 families left with about 1,000 reindeer. "The number of families has fallen because a lot of them have been synthesized with the mainstream community," he says. "Many of them have moved to the towns and even to the capital cities...They want to go down and stay in warm cabins in the winter, maybe buy a car and drive...There's a big appeal to the modern life. The hardships of the traditional life as a reindeer herder certainly play a factor."

Sweeney continues, "To further add to the Dukha's woes, the number of the reindeer they're so dependent on has dwindled dramatically."

That was 2016. Later reports from 2017 and 2018 gave a different view.

There are several folks who have visited the taiga and have intimate knowledge of the culture who provide a positive spin. Morgan Keay, who initiated the Itgel Foundation with musician Liliana Goldman Carrizo with whom I worked, is one. Dan Plumley, at the time the coordinator of the Cultural Survival Peoples Preservation Project, is another. A third, Sas Carey's mission, Nomadicare, "supports and preserves traditional Mongolian nomadic culture through healthcare, films, and stories."

Sas keeps up with individual herders and documents their lives. She takes hygiene kits and vitamins. She also started a database that she gave to each family, the soum doctor and the Ministry of Health. She probably knows the people and their culture better than any foreigner.

In the spring of 2019, Plumley told me that there are currently 1,500 reindeer. Keay confirmed that figure two months later and added that a big celebration was planned for 2020 when the herd was expected to reach 2,000 head.

While Ulysse Girard's report on the condition of the TCVC is damning, his 2017 visit to both east and west taiga provided a wealth of detail about the Tsaatan and their reindeer. There are 44 families (some 220 folks) living in the region. The average herd size was just over 37 animals, making a sum total of 1,641 head, a figure that resembles those reported by both Plumley and Keay.

He wrote that tourism has become a major income earner for many families, but it comes as no surprise that the number of tourist visits to camps varies between 200 and only two. The more remote the camp, the fewer the visits.

While almost all families expressed the feeling that there "would never be too much tourism," Girard noted that tourists significantly

> changed the camp landscape, they were pretty aggressively chasing for pictures of typical nomad life. I noticed during the wedding ceremony that occurred during our stay that the intensity of tourist's eagerness for photography did insult some Tsaatan persons at some points.

In this regard he echoed Rebecca Watters's observations, mentioned above, of bad behaviour by tourists, including just barging into houses (urts).

Girard reported that the main income for the families comes in the form of government subsidies that, for the average family, supplies the bulk of income at seven million tugriks (US$2,681). Other sources include guiding, artwork sales, renting urts space to visitors and blueberry and pine nut sales. These add up to 1.5 million tugriks, which brings the annual income to US$3,250.

Almost 40 per cent of the families now own houses in Tsagaan Nuur. This allows mothers and children to stay in town during the school year.

There are several issues that are of concern. Most are related to the ban on hunting and the related embargo on fishing and cutting of trees, although the last-named can be carried out with a permit. The hunting veto goes beyond food. Another issue Girard wrote of was that "the prohibition of wolf hunts is a serious issue because of wolf attacks. On average, the annual loss for each of the 44 families is three reindeer. One family lost twelve animals in a single year."

Other concerns expressed by a few families included the loss of the Tuvan language, diseases of the deer and the lack of availability of drugs for treatment, poor quality of Chinese-made clothing and the problems of access to health care.

One sad matter is alcohol consumption. Girard learned of it, but only in one-to-one, very private and unofficial discussions. He most often saw drunken people in Tsagaan Nuur. Acute alcohol poisoning led to the death of some of the men I'd met during my own time in the taiga.

This part of the report shows a parallel between the changes in the Indigenous cultures of Canada and that of the Tsaatan.

> Communities initially live a nomadic life on trad-
> itional territories; valuable natural resources are
> found in the area; money is offered to nomads;
> nomads slowly give up traditional way of life and
> switch to sedentary life; psychological distress,
> alcohol, drugs and violence problems come in.

A further subject, climate change, is impacting the reindeer. Between 2016 and 2018, William Taylor and his colleagues rode into the west taiga and interviewed families about the changes in ice conditions. The people have traditionally relied on areas of ice that do not melt in summer for use as resting places that give their animals respite from the heat. The ice also keeps insects at bay. These patches have steadily begun to melt in recent years. This has led to threats to the health of the reindeer, the condition of summer pastures and the need for the urgent changes to long-established management systems of the herds.

In 1963 Bob Dylan wrote his famous song, "The Times They Are A-Changin'." For domestic reindeer herding cultures, they are indeed a-changin'.

CHAPTER 27

COVID

Where a major component of the domestic reindeer activity relied on tourism, all was fine and dandy up until the Christmas season of 2019.

Then came COVID-19.

The full extent of the impact of the pandemic was not initially recognized. As the world began to accept the seriousness of the situation, for the reindeer industry everything changed.

Of course, much more drastic consequences hit people and businesses in orders of magnitude greater than reindeer operations, especially the domestic ones. When the infection was better understood, virtually all tourism the world over came to a crashing halt.

For the reindeer people, most local and tourist activities ceased. Father Christmas parades, reindeer rides (on saddles or sleighs), photo opportunities, yoga classes and supermarket visits — all came to a standstill. Travel restrictions, quarantine, lockdown, spiralling infection rates and social distancing meant that few, if any, tourists were able, or willing, to visit any place where a risk of contact with other humans or even some animal species known to carry the corona virus could occur. These activities may recover, albeit slowly, when the pandemic is under control and an effective vaccine becomes widely available.

Three examples tell the tale.

The Cairngorm Reindeer Herd in Scotland, whose ancestors were imported in 1952 from Sweden, thrived until the pandemic hit. The enterprise, near Aviemore in the Scottish Highlands, like others, derived most of its income from parades. When restrictions were imposed, the tourists vanished overnight.

The owners and dedicated staff team members involved made an inspired choice. On March 22, 2020, they posted this on their website:

> In light of current developments, we will unfortunately be completely closed to the public as of 23rd March 2020. As the situation is so unknown, we cannot currently give a date for reopening, but hopefully we will survive long enough to be able to open again once restrictions are lifted, whenever that may be.
>
> Without our Hill Trips, the bulk of our income, vital to the upkeep of the herd, has vanished. We appreciate that these are incredibly difficult times for everyone, but if you do feel able to financially support us, please consider adopting a reindeer. As with the Foot-and-Mouth outbreak in 2001, which forced us to close temporarily, it's times like these that the adoption scheme is vital to our survival as a business.
>
> We have also set up a donate button, if you would like to support us with a one-off amount of your choice.

I contacted Cairngorm again 13 months after the lockdown, after reading one of their Facebook posts, to learn more details. The reply I received is a testament to both the hard work they put in to keep the business going, and the popularity of the enterprise. Andi, a member of the team, wrote, "Like most non-essential businesses in Scotland, April 26th was the magic date in our roadmap back to 'normality' that we were allowed to reopen." She also wrote, "The adoption scheme is hugely important to us and kept us going through COVID. We have had hundreds of people choose to support us by adopting a reindeer during the pandemic. Over 32,000 people follow our Facebook page, so it's not unusual to receive over 1,000 likes on a post — some videos go viral and receive over 100,000 views. Why? Well, who doesn't love photos of reindeer?!"

In Finland the pandemic has affected the reindeer culture far beyond the visits and rides. Over six million tourists used to visit the country every year. Trips to Lapland were very much part of the experience, especially in winter. An ice castle hotel was built every year and the northern lights can be seen upwards of 150 nights a year from Rovaniemi. The town was declared the official home of Santa Claus in 1985 and markets more than the opportunity to see the aurora borealis. There is Santa's Post Office, SantaPark — a Christmas theme park and Santa Claus Village. All of these tourist opportunities are no longer part of the town's economy. There is more. In March 2020 Anne Ollila wrote this to me:

> In Finland, reindeer meat markets are heavily relying on restaurant sector and the restaurants are now basically closed. Tourism is the biggest customer in restaurants in Lapland, and also tourism is completely off. Reindeer related tourism (sleigh rides, reindeer farm visits, etc.) is also off. So the impacts

to reindeer herding industry are already massive. Yet, I cannot tell how long these impacts will paralyze our livelihood, and how well we can cope. Next autumn will show how deep waters we are swimming.

In the case of Mongolia's would-be tourists, all international flights are suspended and the country's border with China has been closed to land traffic. The flight ban has shut down all foreign visits to the Tsaatan homelands. This has had a negative impact on the nomads who have enjoyed income from those visits. In late April 2020, Byamba replied to my question about the situation in Mongolia. He wrote, "It's tough. No spread in general public, but the economy is suffering. No tours, lockdown. Running on reserves."

Epilogue

The careers of the folks I worked with on caribou in Canada's Saskatchewan and Albertan wilderness have changed. Jon Jorgensen is a researcher with Alberta Fish and Wildlife. Jim Rettie runs a private consulting company based in Winnipeg. Tom Hauge retired after 25 years with the Wisconsin Department of Natural Resources.

When it comes to domestic reindeer, there have been several changes in the intervening years. The domestic and semi-domestic herd situation varies from place to place. With the exception of the Scandinavian industry that mainly focuses on the meat market, large-scale, semi-domestic herding has been in decline for several years. In Russia and Alaska, the cultures are starting to vanish as the number of animals decreases. In Mongolia, where there are significant numbers of reindeer, the culture is thriving.

In Finland, where I had the good fortune to join Mauri Nieminen and Dr. Timo Soveri during one of their research trips to Kaamanen in 1991, Mauri has retired, and Timo has gone on from his assistant professorship at the veterinary school to professor of ruminant medicine at the University of Helsinki. Sadly, my friend Harry Jalanka died after a surgery went wrong.

Also, in Finland, field slaughter like that I'd witnessed in 1991 is no longer permitted. Slaughterhouses are strictly regulated and must conform to EU directives. The rules apply to all, from large-scale, commercial operations to private, small-scale ones.

Among those with whom I worked in Mongolia, Morgan Keay has retained her interest in the culture but has not been actively involved for several years. She is CEO and founder of Motive International, a global social enterprise.

Jason Johns is a biologist/ecologist science support technician who works in remote locations. His trip to Mongolia was just the start of a career that has taken him to many regions, almost to the ends of the earth. These include the Palmer Station in Antarctica, Greenland and Arctic Alaska. When his work took him to Samoa, his days off no doubt involved beach wear rather than a down parka and other essential cold weather gear.

Liliana Goldman Carrizo has continued with her musical life. Following her time in Mongolia and trips to India, Iraq and Europe, she returned to the United States, where she completed degrees, both an MA and PhD, in ethnomusic. After a period as a postdoctoral fellow in the humanities at Harvard University, she accepted a position as an assistant professor of ethnomusicology at Colorado College. She continues to support the Dad'suren School for Traditional Music.

Bill Coyle continues to run his turf business in Colorado.

Meagan Flenniken changed her 2005 career goal of veterinary medicine and is now a physician and the mother of 2-year-old James.

Greg Finstad remains the program manager for the Reindeer Research Program in Alaska.

Sas Carey, who has returned to visit Mongolia nearly every year, told me about some of the people I met and worked with.

Ganbat, one of the two veterinary technicians who accompanied us in the taiga, is now a respected sage in the community. He said, "The reindeer is the most important thing in our lives; if there were no reindeer, we would not exist." His statement echoes what Sanjim said to Morgan in 2002. Borkhuu, the other vet tech, works in Tsagaan Nuur.

Erdenchimeg, whom I watched milking a reindeer, still lives in the west taiga with her grown children.

Some other Tsaatan are no longer alive. Among them the shamans Ghosta, Soyan, who treated my swollen arm, and blind Tsend. Also no longer with us is JBat, who hosted me with such friendliness despite our almost complete lack of a common language.

Other Mongolians include Bayanmunk, who continues with his wrangling work, and Byamba, who joined with colleagues (one his wife) to form their own company serving the tourist industry in general (www.wandermongolia.com). He has kept up his contacts with the reindeer herders, most recently guiding a group to the east taiga.

Sadly, I never heard from Khosbayar, so I don't know if she completed her studies and graduated. I hope so, because she could be not only a woman vet but a useful link between the Tsaatan culture and other Mongolians.

In Ulaanbaatar several things have changed since my last trip in 2006. In 2018 Jan Wigsten wrote and told me that the strange statues of the lion and the lion woman chimera are still there, but the entire children's park has been taken over by the city's only five-star hotel, the Shangri La. Inside the garden the amazing Tumen Ekh ensemble that mesmerized me still performs outstanding folk shows, but the park has been newly built and moved to the south in order to give way for the hotel. He wrote that it is now a better venue. Chez Bernard, the cafe frequented by expats where I enjoyed my breakfasts, is long gone. The competition for similar venues is now fierce, with many smart places for coffee. No Starbucks yet.

The road to Murun is now tarred, an improvement to the multi-hour-long trip over nonexistent roads.

The massive change in Mongolia's Tsaatan culture that occurred in 2011, when the government established Tengis-Shishged National Park, has led to further changes. As I noted in Chapter 26, the Tsaatan were banned from hunting or fishing, but in 2019 Byamba wrote, "In Shishged and Tengis confluence there are fly fishing camps and under a jealously guarded licensing foreign tourists are allowed to fly fish."

A 2017 survey involving interviews with the families and studies of their deer revealed that tourism has become a major source of income but that this change has been accompanied by its own problems. The survey also provided encouraging news of increase in the herd size.

There are ups and downs to the reindeer story. The wild herds are in sharp decline everywhere. While the natural ebb and flow of population sizes is part of the story, the role of humans, and what we are doing to so many natural systems across the planet, continues to upset the balance.

Acknowledgements

I am indebted to many people with whom I worked in the field and to those who answered my questions and helped me get the facts straight.

In particular, Dr. Greg Finstad gave me many insights about the global reindeer industry. Dr. Nicholas Tyler not only told me about the Uganda kob Rudolph avatar but also guided me on the biology of, and the impacts upon, reindeer life. Mauri Nieminen guided me on an exciting new path. Anne Ollila generously shared numerous aspects of the reindeer in Finland and, through her colleagues, sent me many wonderful photos. Byamba, Jan Wigsten and Sas Carey were mines of information about many aspects of Mongolian culture and the lives of the Tsaatan. Dr. Helen Schwantje updated me on the situation in British Columbia.

Thanks also to the many herders who welcomed me and were generous in their hospitality when we visited their homes.

Others who freely offered vital input are Birgitta Åhman, Dr. Hezy Anholt, Dr. Greg Appleyard, Dr. John Blake, Bayanmunk, Borkhuu, Dr. Stan Bychawski, Randy Capsell, Dr. Meagan Chambers, Allan Coukell, Bill Coyle, Dr. Robert Dieterich,

Janchivdorj Erdenebaatar, Dr. John Fletcher, Ganbat, Teresa Gaskill, Bob Gerlach, Vicki Gerwing, Dr. Liliana Goldman Carrizo, Dr. Janet Hill, Jeremy Hsieh, Mike Jablonski, Anna-Leena Jänkälä, Jason Johns, Jon Jorgensen, Aare Jortikka, Tarja Konstig, Jouko Kumpula, Sauli Laaksonen, Clayton Lamb, Danica Lorer, Dr. Amélie Mathieu, Bruce McLellan, Dr. Dick Neal, Dr. Milla Niemi, Dr. Kirk Olson, Antti Paasivaara, Lincoln Parret, Dr. Yves Plante, Dan Plumley, Dr. Marjatta Rantala, Fran Rees, Dr. Jim Rettie, Hen Robinson, Dr. Knut Röed, Dr. Jan Rowell, Jim Schaefer, Teresa Sigafoose, Tilly Smith, Dr. Timo Soveri, Dr. Paul Stevens, Dr. Stacy Tessaro, Dr. David Waltner-Toews, Paige Wark, Dr. Rebecca Watters, Dr. Doug Whiteside, Charlene Wirtz, Dr. Murray Woodbury, Simon Youé and Dr. Petra Ziegler.

Dr. Amélie Mathieu and Tayyab Shah used their expertise with the maps. Without those, the work would have been incomplete.

Of course, I am indebted to Morgan Keay for the chance to travel to Mongolia and learn about the nomadic culture of hardy and hospitable people.

Screening and editing are crucial elements of any writing. My wife and best friend Jo looked at every chapter and patiently suggested changes, as well as spotted many typos. The members of my writing group took the next step and suggested changes and ways to improve the work. Those who were with me on the journey are Charlene Blackwell, Jean Heal, Judy McCrosky, Jeanette Montgomery, Murray Lindsay, Larry Strome and Charlene Wirtz.

Editor and author Meaghan Craven cast her eagle eye over the text and made many suggestions on early chapters. Thanks Meaghan.

Thanks to Don Gorman and his team at Rocky Mountain Books, especially my editor Kirsten Craven whose eagle eye and attention to detail were crucial to the enterprise. It has been a privilege and pleasure to work with her.

Selected Sources

Chapter 1: New Beginnings

Banfield, A.W.F. *The Mammals of Canada*. Toronto: University of Toronto Press, 1974.

Chapter 2: The Santa Story and Rudolph's Nose

BMJ. "Why Rudolph's Nose Is Red." *YouTube*. https://www.youtube.com/watch?v=Iro_WBt-d_Y.

The Cairngorm Reindeer Herd: Roaming Freely since 1952. http://www.cairngormreindeer.co.uk/.

Evans, O.L. "Why Reindeer Noses Are More Amazing Than You Think." *BBC Earth*, December 9, 2015. http://www.bbc.com/earth/story/20151209-why-reindeer-noses-are-more-amazing-than-you-think.

Hemmings, J. "The Russian Reindeer Who Served on a British Sub." *War History Online*, March 24, 2019. https://www.warhistoryonline.com/instant-articles/pollyanna-the-reindeer-wwii.html.

Ince, C., et al. "Why Rudolph's Nose Is Red: Observational Study." *BMJ*, December 17, 2012. doi: https://doi.org/10.1136/bmj.e8311.

Lewis, D. "Rudolph the Red Knows Undersea Warfare, Dear." *Now I Know That's Half the Battle*, June 18, 2019. http://nowiknow.com/ rudolph-the-red-knows-undersea-warfare-dear/.

"Reindeer's Wartime Submarine Trip." *BBC News*, December 21, 2009. http:// news.bbc.co.uk/local/hampshire/hi/people_and_places/history/ newsid_8386000/8386947.stm.

"Royal Navy Reindeer Submariner's Starring Role on BBC's *The One Show*." *The National Museum, Royal Navy*. https://www.nmrn.org.uk/news-events/nmrn-blog/ royal-navy-reindeer-submariner's-starring-role-bbc's-one-show.

Chapter 3: Reindeer Domestication

Clutton-Brock, J. "The Process of Domestication." *Mammal Review* 22, no. 2 (1992): 79–85. https://doi.org/10.1111/j.1365-2907.1992.tb00122.x.

"Domestication." *National Geographic Society*. https://www.nationalgeo-graphic.org/encyclopedia/domestication/.

Fletcher, T.J. *Deer*. London, UK: Reaktion Books Ltd., 2014.

———. "Farmed Deer: New Domestic Animals Defined by Controlled Breeding." *Reproduction Fertility and Development* 13, no. 7–8 (2001): 511–516. https://www.researchgate.net/publication/11372102_Farmed_deer_New_domestic_animals_defined_by_controlled_breeding.

Jones, L. "A Soviet Scientist Created the Only Tame Foxes in the World." *BBC Earth*, September 13, 2016. http://www.bbc.com/earth/story/20160912-a-soviet-scientist-created-the-only-tame-foxes-in-the-world.

Koenig, R. "Move Over, Goat Yoga. Alaskans Now Have Reindeer Yoga." *NPR*, June 22, 2019. https://www.npr.org/2019/06/22/733849625/ move-over-goat-yoga-alaskans-now-have-reindeer-yoga.

Lopatin, I.A. "The Extinct and Near Extinct Tribes of Northeastern Asia as Compared with the American Indian." *American Antiquity* 5, no. 3 (January 1940): 202–208. https://www.cambridge.org/core/journals/american-antiquity/article/extinct-and-nearextinct-tribes-of-northeastern-asia-as-compared-with-the-american-indian/966F1D0C890519CB-C963AB3E1B19A413.

Schefferus, J. *Lapponia, id est regionis Lapponum et gentis nova et verissima descriptio.* Francofurti, 1673.

Smith, T. *The Real Rudolph: A Natural History of Reindeer.* Stroud, UK: Sutton Publishing Ltd., 2006.

Vitebsky, P. *The Reindeer People: Living with Animals and Spirits in Siberia.* New York: Harper Collins, 2005.

Chapter 4: Traditional Tales

Ernits, E. *Folktales of Meandash, The Mythic Sami Reindeer.* https://www.folklore.ee/folklore/vol13/meandash.htm.

Keay, M.G. "The Tsaatan Reindeer Herders of Mongolia: Forgotten Lessons of Human-Animal Systems." *Encyclopedia of Animals and Humans,* 2006.

Chapter 5: Caribou in Canada

Spears, R.A. *McGraw-Hill's Dictionary of American Idioms and Phrasal Verbs.* New York: The McGraw-Hill Companies, Inc., 2002.

Chapter 6: A Visit to Finland

Jalanka, H. "Management of Norwegian lemmings *Lemmus lemmus.*" *Proceedings of the American Association of Zoo Veterinarians,* 1988.

Chapter 7: Finland's Reindeer Industry

Barth, B. "Growing Horsetail Plants." *Love to Know.* https://garden.lovetoknow.com/lawns-ornamental-grasses/growing-horsetail-plants.

Patterson, S. "Horsetail Plants: How to Get Rid of Horsetail Weeds."
    https://www.gardeningknowhow.com/edible/herbs/horsetail/horse-
    tail-weed-control.htm.

Chapter 11: Towards the Taiga

Koffman, M. "Curried Soul." *YouTube*. http://www.youtube.com/
    watch?v=KjTnwmHbwDc.

Chapter 14: First Reindeer

Araj, G.F., et al. "Assessment of Brucellosis Card Test in Screening Patients for
    Brucellosis." *Epidemiology & Infection* 100, no. 3 (1988): 389–398. https://
    www.ncbi.nlm.nih.gov/pmc/articles/PMC2249350/.

Chapter 16: Off West

Roberts, C. "Why Are Girl Babies Winning in the Battle for Survival?" *The
    University of Adelaide News & Events*, May 28, 2014. https://www.
    adelaide.edu.au/news/news70802.html.

Chapter 17: A Second Year

Oksanen, A., et al. "Oral and Parenteral Administration of Ivermectin to
    Reindeer." *Veterinary Parasitology* 41, no. 3–4 (March 1992): 241–247.
    https://www.ncbi.nlm.nih.gov/pubmed/1502787.

Chapter 18: A Shaman's Treatment

Equine Brucellosis. https://www.addl.purdue.edu/newsletters/1994/equin-
    ebruc.shtml.

Chapter 19: Year Three in Mongolia

Haigh, J.C., et al. "A Novel Clinical Syndrome and Detection of Anaplasma
    Ovis in Mongolian Reindeer (*Rangifer tarandus*)." *Journal of Wildlife
    Diseases* 44, no. 3 (July 2008): 569–577. https://www.ncbi.nlm.nih.gov/
    pubmed/18689641.

Chapter 22: The Artificial Insemination Issue

Atkin, C. "Russian Military Trains Using Reindeer and Sled Dogs in -30C Cold." *Independent*, February 2, 2016. https://www.independent.co.uk/news/world/europe/video-russian-military-trains-reindeer-husky-sled-dogs-30c-cold-a6848551.html.

Haigh, J.C., and R.J. Hudson. *Farming Wapiti and Red Deer*. Maryland Heights, MO: Mosby, 1993.

Olson, K., et al. "Wildlife Availability as a Reason for Decline of Domestic Reindeer in North Western Mongolia." Unpublished paper, 2006.

Røed, K., et al. "Genetic Distinctiveness of Isolated and Threatened Tsaatan Reindeer Herds in Mongolia." *Proceedings of the 6th International Deer Biology Congress*, Prague, Czech Republic, 2006.

Chapter 23: Disease Studies

Araj, G.F., et al. "Assessment of Brucellosis Card Test in Screening Patients for Brucellosis." *Epidemiology & Infection* 100, no. 3 (1988): 389–398. https://www.ncbi.nlm.nih.gov/pmc/articles/PMC2249350/.

Dieterich, R.A., et al. "Effects of Killed *Brucella abortus* Strain 45/20 Vaccine on Reindeer Later Challenge Exposed with *Brucella suis* Type 4." *American Journal of Veterinary Research* 42, no. 1 (January 1981): 131–134. https://pubmed.ncbi.nlm.nih.gov/6784617/.

———. "Observations on Reindeer Vaccinated with *Brucella melitensis* Strain H-38 Vaccine and Challenged with *Brucella suis* Type 4." *Proceedings of the 2nd International Reindeer/Caribou Symposium*, Røros, Norway, 1979.

Dieterich, R.A., and J.K. Morton. "Effects of Live *Brucella abortus* Strain 19 Vaccine on Reindeer." *Rangifer* 9, no. 2 (January 2010): 47–50. https://www.researchgate.net/publication/45437119_Effects_of_live_Brucella_abortus_strain_19vaccine_on_reindeer.

Dieterich, R.A., and J.K. Morton. "Effects of Live *Brucella abortus* Strain 19 Vaccine on Reindeer Later Challenge Exposed with *Brucella suis* Type 4." *Rangifer* 7, no. 1 (January 2010): 33–36. https://www.researchgate.net/publication/45437055_Effects_of_live_Brucella_abortus_strain_19vaccine_on_reindeer_later_challenge_exposed_with_Brucella_suis_type_4.

Erdenebaatar, J., et al. "Epidemiological and Serological Survey of Brucellosis in Mongolia by ELISA Using Sarcosine Extracts." *Microbiology and Immunology* 48, no. 8 (2004): 571–577. https://pubmed.ncbi.nlm.nih.gov/15322336/.

Morton, J.K. "Laboratory and Field Trials of Killed *Brucella suis* Type 4 Vaccine in Reindeer." *Fifth International Reindeer/Caribou Symposium*, Arvidsjaur, Sweden, 1988. https://septentrio.uit.no/index.php/rangifer/article/view/878.

———. "Role of Predators in Reindeer Brucellosis in Alaska." *Rangifer* 6, Special Issue no. 1 (1986): 368. https://septentrio.uit.no/index.php/rangifer/article/view/682.

Olson, K.A., et al. "Genetic Diversity and Decline of Domesticated Reindeer of the Dukha in North Western Mongolia." Unpublished paper, 2004.

Papageorgiou, S., et al. "Detection and Epidemiology of Tick-Borne Pathogens in Free-Ranging Livestock in Mongolia." *Journal of Clinical & Experimental Pathology*, Special Issue (2012). https://www.omicsonline.org/detection-and-epidemiology-of-tick-borne-pathogens-in-free-ranging-livestock-in-mongolia-2161-0681.S3-006.php?aid=11142.

———. "First Detection of *Borrelia* spp. in Mongolian Reindeer." 57th Annual Wildlife Disease Association Conference, Edmonton, Alberta, 2008.

Rausch, R. "Brucellosis in Reindeer, *Rangifer tarandus* L., Inoculated Experimentally with *Brucella suis*, Type 4." *Canadian Journal of Microbiology* 24, no. 2 (1978): 129–135. https://pubmed.ncbi.nlm.nih.gov/647470/.

Vitebsky, P. *The Reindeer People: Living with Animals and Spirits in Siberia.* New York: Harper Collins, 2005.

Chapter 24: Predator Problems

Damages Caused by Carnivores. Finnish Reindeer Herders' Association. https://paliskunnat.fi/reindeer-herders-association/reindeer-damages/predator-damages/.

Gustine, D.D., et al. "Calf Survival of Woodland Caribou in a Multi-Predator Ecosystem." *Wildlife Monographs* 165, no. 1 (December 2006): 1–32. http://dx.doi.org/10.2193/0084-0173(2006)165[1:CSOWCI]2.0.CO;2.

"How Poaching Is 'Killing Off' the World's Largest Reindeer Herd on Taimyr Peninsula." *The Siberian Times*, February 7, 2017. https://siberiantimes. com/ecology/casestudy/features/f0285-how-poaching-is-killing-off-the-worlds-largest-reindeer-herd-on-taimyr-peninsula/.

Klemensson, V. "How Wolverines Kill Reindeers." *YouTube*. https://www. youtube.com/watch?v=okpKzPxwo_M.

Magoun, A.J., et al. "Predation on Caribou (*Rangifer tarandus*) by Wolverines (*Gulo gulo*) after Long Pursuits." *Canadian Field Naturalist* 132, no. 4 (July 2019): 382. https://www.researchgate.net/publication/334445575_ Predation_on_Caribou_Rangifer_tarandus_by_Wolverines_Gulo_ gulo_after_long_pursuits.

Owen, J. "'Reindeer People' Resort to Eating Their Herds." *National Geographic News*, November 4, 2004. https://news.nationalgeographic. com/news/2004/11/1104_041104_reindeer_people.html.

"Shocking New Evidence of 'Mass Murder' of Famous Reindeer Population." *The Siberian Times*, April 14, 2017. https://siberiantimes.com/other/ others/news/shocking-new-evidence-of-mass-murder-of-famous-rein-deer-population/.

Stewart, R.R. "Bears Get a Free Pass to the Caribou Zoo." *Alberta Outdoors*, October 2018. https://www.academia.edu/37618791/ Bears_Get_A_Free_Pass_To_The_Caribou_Zoo.

Vitebsky, P. *The Reindeer People: Living with Animals and Spirits in Siberia*. New York: Harper Collins, 2005.

"Wolverine's Diet and Hunting Behaviour." *SUURPEDOT.FI*. http://www. largecarnivores.fi/species/wolverine/wolverines-diet-and-hunting-be-haviour.html.

Zager, P., and J. Beecham. "The Role of American Black Bears and Brown Bears as Predators on Ungulates in North America." *Ursus* 17, no. 2 (2006): 95–108. https://www.academia.edu/28666139/The_role_of_ American_black_bears_and_brown_bears_as_predators_on_ungu-lates_in_North_America?auto=download.

Chapter 25: Declines and Crashes of Caribou and Wild Reindeer

Anderson, T.A., and C.J. Johnson. "Distribution of Barren-Ground Caribou during Winter in Response to Fire." *Ecosphere* 5, no. 10 (2014): 140. https://doi.org/10.1890/ES14-00010.1.

The Associated Press. "Winnipeg Show Exhibits Rarely Seen Images of 1950s Arctic Famine." *CP24*, December 5, 2009. https://www.cp24.com/winnipeg-show-exhibits-rarely-seen-images-of-1950s-arctic-famine-1.461570.

Avery, H. "Moving North to Survive." *CBC News*, March 31, 2019. https://newsinteractives.cbc.ca/longform/moving-north-to-survive.

Barker, R. "What Extinction in Idaho Looks Like: Last Caribou Captured, Ending Conservation Program." *Idaho Statesman*, March 1, 2019. https://www.idahostatesman.com/news/local/news-columns-blogs/letters-from-the-west/article226870904.html.

Baskin, L. "Number of Wild and Domestic Reindeer in Russia in the Late 20th Century." *Rangifer* 25, no. 1 (January 2010): 51–57. https://www.researchgate.net/publication/43296991_Number_of_wild_and_domestic_reindeer_in_Russia_in_the_late_20th_century.

"A Brighter Future for Caribou." *Caribou Conservation Breeding Foundation* (CCBF). https://www.ccbf.ca.

Burch, Jr., E.S. "The Caribou/Wild Reindeer as a Human Resource." *American Antiquity* 37, no. 3 (July 1972): 339–368. https://www.jstor.org/stable/278435.

"Caribou Habitat Restoration Projects Approved." *British Columbia Information Bulletin*, July 16, 2020. https://archive.news.gov.bc.ca/releases/news_releases_2017-2021/2020FLNR0040-001286.htm.

Compton, B., et al. "Survival and Mortality of Translocated Woodland Caribou." *Wildlife Society Bulletin* 23 (1995): 490–496.

COSEWIC Assessment and Update Status Report on the Peary Caribou Rangifer tarandus pearyi and Barren-Ground Caribou Rangifer tarandus groenlandicus in Canada, 2004. https://www.sararegistry.gc.ca/virtual_sara/files/cosewic/sr_peary_caribou_e.pdf.

Cox, S. "BC Government to Auction Off Old-Growth in Critical Habitat for Endangered Caribou." *The Narwhal*, October 8, 2020. https://thenarwhal.ca/bc-old-growth-logging-endangered-caribou-habitat/?utm_source=The+Narwhal+Newsletter&utm_campaign=31411817cf-Oct+15+2020+—+Newsletter+—+non-members&utm_medium=email&utm_term=0_f6a05fddb8-31411817cf-108584788.

Dall, W.H. *Alaska and Its Resources*. Boston: Lee and Shepard, 1897.

DeCesare, N., et al. "The Role of Translocation in Recovery of Woodland Caribou Populations." *Conservation Biology* 25 (2011): 365–373.

Environment Canada. *Recovery Strategy for the Woodland Caribou, Southern Mountain Population* (Rangifer tarandus caribou) *in Canada*. Ottawa: Environment Canada, 2014. https://www.registrelep-sararegistry.gc.ca/virtual_sara/files/plans/rs_woodland_caribou_bois_s_mtn_pop_0114_e.pdf.

Gauthier, M., and R. Pravettoni. "'We have nothing but our reindeer': Conservation Threatens Ruination for Mongolia's Dukha." *The Guardian*, August 28, 2016. https://www.theguardian.com/global-development/2016/aug/28/reindeer-conservation-threatens-ruination-mongolia-dukha.

Government of Canada. *Southern Mountain Caribou in British Columbia: Bilateral Conservation Agreement between Canada and British Columbia*. https://www.canada.ca/en/environment-climate-change/services/species-risk-public-registry/conservation-agreements/southern-mountain-caribou-british-colombia-2020.html#toco.

Haigh, J.C. *The Trouble with Lions*. Edmonton: University of Alberta Press, 2008.

"Hands-On Conservation at the Klinse-Za Caribou Maternity Pen." *Habitat Conservation Trust Foundation*, March 21, 2019. https://hctf.ca/hands-on-conservation-at-the-klinse-za-caribou-maternity-pen/.

Imminent Threat Assessment for Southern Mountain Caribou. Ministry of Environment and Climate Change Canada, 2018. https://www.registrelep-sararegistry.gc.ca/virtual_sara/files/ImminentThreatAnalysisSmc%2Dv00%2D2018Jun%2DEng%2Epdf.

Le Moullec, M., et al. "A Century of Conservation: The Ongoing Recovery of Svalbard Reindeer." *The Journal of Wildlife Management* 83, no. 8 (2019): 1676–1686. https://doi.org/10.1002/jwmg.21761.

Lewis, S. "200 Reindeer Starved to Death in Norway and Scientists Say Climate Change Is to Blame." *CBS News*, August 3, 2019. https://www.cbsnews.com/news/reindeer-dead-norway-200-starved-to-death-svalbard-scientists-blame-climate-change/.

McLellan, B.N. *An Historic Perspective of Mountain Caribou Distribution and Abundance.* Columbia Mountains Caribou Research Project, 2010. https://cmu.abmi.ca/wp-content/uploads/2017/09/McLellan-History-of-Mountain-Caribou4.pdf.

Mihai, A. "A Christmas Tragedy: The Arctic Has Lost 2.6 Million Reindeer over the Past 20 Years." *ZME Science*, August 13, 2019. https://www.zmescience.com/science/fewer-reindeer-20122018/.

Mizin, I. *The Current State of the Wild Reindeer in Russia: General Overview of the Situation.* World Wildlife Fund, 2018. https://carma.caff.is/images/_Organized/CARMA/About/Conferences/Carma9/3._Ivan_Reindeer_presentation_CARMA9-2.pdf.

Mullaney, T. "Trump Rushes to Lock Down Oil Drilling in Alaska's Arctic National Wildlife Refuge before Biden Takes Office." *CNBC*, December 4, 2020. https://www.cnbc.com/2020/12/04/trump-rushes-drilling-in-arctic-wildlife-reserve-before-biden-takes-office.html.

Northwest Territories. *Barren-Ground Caribou Habitat and Fire*, 2018. https://www.enr.gov.nt.ca/sites/enr/files/resources/caribou_fire_fs_en.pdf.

Northwest Territories Species at Risk Committee. *Species Status Report Porcupine Caribou and Barren-Ground Caribou in the Northwest Territories*, April 2017. https://www.nwtspeciesatrisk.ca/sites/enr-species-at-risk/files/bgc_and_pch_status_report_and_assessment_final_apr1117.pdf.

Porcupine Caribou Management Board. https://www.pcmb.ca/herd.

Quinn, E. "Inuit Government Calls to Respect Ban on Caribou Harvest in Atlantic Canada." *Eye on the Arctic. Radio Canada International*, January 31, 2020. https://www.rcinet.ca/en/2020/01/31/inuit-government-calls-to-respect-ban-on-caribou-harvest-in-atlantic-canada/.

Ray, J. "At Risk of Extinction." *Canadian Geographic*, October 31, 2018. https://www.canadiangeographic.ca/article/risk-extinction.

Rennie, S. "Hunger in the Arctic." *The Canadian Press*, 2015. http://cponline.thecanadianpress.com/graphics/2015/hunger-in-the-arctic/indexm.html.

Rettie, J., and F. Messier. "Dynamics of Woodland Caribou Populations at the Southern Limit of Their Range in Saskatchewan." *Canadian Journal of Zoology* 76, no. 2 (February 1998). https://cdnsciencepub.com/doi/abs/10.1139/z97-193.

Russell, D.E., A. Gunn, and S. Kutz. "Migratory Tundra Caribou and Wild Reindeer." *Arctic Report Card: Update for 2018.* National Oceanic and Atmospheric Administration. https://arctic.noaa.gov/Report-Card/Report-Card-2018/ArtMID/7878/ArticleID/784/Migratory-Tundra-Caribou-and-Wild-Reindeer.

Skoog, R.O. "Ecology of the caribou (*Rangifer tarandus granti*) in Alaska." PhD diss., University of California, Berkeley, 1968. https://www.arlis.org/docs/vol2/hydropower/APA_DOC_no._2578.pdf.

Storeheier, P., et al. "Nutritive Value of Terricolous Lichens for Reindeer in Winter." *The Lichenologist* 34, no. 3 (May 2002): 247–257. https://doi.org/10.1006/lich.2002.0394.

Struzik, E. "A Troubling Decline in the Caribou Herds of the Arctic." *Yale Environment 360*, September 23, 2010. https://e360.yale.edu/features/a_troubling_decline_in_the_caribou_herds_of_the_arctic.

Tyler, N.J.C. "Climate, Snow, Ice, Crashes, and Declines in Populations of Reindeer and Caribou (*Rangifer tarandus L.*)." *Ecological Monographs*, Ecological Society of America 80, no. 2 (May 2010): 197–219. https://esajournals.onlinelibrary.wiley.com/doi/10.1890/09-1070.1.

US Fish and Wildlife Service. *Kenai National Wildlife Refuge, Alaska.* https://www.fws.gov/refuge/Kenai/what_we_do/resource_management/caribou.html.

Vors, L.S., and M.S. Boyce. "Global Declines of Caribou and Reindeer." *Global Change Biology* 15, no. 11 (November 2009): 2626–2633. https://onlinelibrary.wiley.com/doi/abs/10.1111/j.1365-2486.2009.01974.x.

Chapter 26: Domestic Reindeer Ups and Downs

Avery, H. "Moving North to Survive." *CBC News*, March 31, 2019. https://
newsinteractives.cbc.ca/longform/moving-north-to-survive.

Baskin, L. "Number of Wild and Domestic Reindeer in Russia in the Late 20th
Century." *Rangifer* 25, no. 1 (January 2010): 51–57. https://www.research-
gate.net/publication/43296991_Number_of_wild_and_domestic_rein-
deer_in_Russia_in_the_late_20th_century.

Chang, E. "The Totem Peoples Preservation Project of Siberia and Mongolia."
Cultural Survival Quarterly Magazine, September 1999. https://
www.culturalsurvival.org/publications/cultural-survival-quarterly/
totem-peoples-preservation-project-siberia-and-mongolia.

Chen, D.H. "Mongolia's Reindeer Herders Defend Their Way of Life."
Aljazeera, March 18, 2017. https://www.aljazeera.com/indepth/fea-
tures/2017/03/mongolia-reindeer-herders-defend-life-170315082203586.
html.

Cook, J. "Norway Sami Community Fights for Survival as Temperatures
Rise." *BBC News*, September 3, 2019. https://www.bbc.com/news/
world-europe-49482095.

Donahue, B. 2003. "The Troubled Taiga." *Cultural Survival Quarterly*,
March 2003. https://www.culturalsurvival.org/publications/
cultural-survival-quarterly/troubled-taiga.

Gauthier, M., and R. Pravettoni. "'We have nothing but our reindeer': Conservation Threatens Ruination for Mongolia's
Dukha." *The Guardian*, August 28, 2016. https://www.
theguardian.com/global-development/2016/aug/28/
reindeer-conservation-threatens-ruination-mongolia-dukha.

Girard, U. *Assessment of Tsaatan Community & Visitors Center: Final Report*,
2018.

———. *The Economic Reality of Tsaatan Families: Economic Survey — Final
Report*, 2018.

Henley, J. "Sweden to Build Reindeer Bridges over Roads and Railways." *The Guardian*, January 20, 2021. https://www.theguardian.com/world/2021/jan/20/ sweden-to-build-bridges-for-reindeer-to-safely-cross-roads-and-railways.

Henry, L.A., et al. "Corporate Social Responsibility and the Oil Industry in the Russian Arctic: Global Norms and Neo-Paternalism." *Europe-Asia Studies* 68, no. 8 (2016). http://dx.doi.org/10.1080/09668136.2016.12335 23.

———. *Reindeer, Oil, and Climate Change: Pressures on the Nenets Indigenous People of the Russian Arctic.* National Council for Eurasian and East European Research, December 30, 2013. https://www.ucis.pitt.edu/ nceeer/2013_827-06_Henry_2.pdf.

Jernsletten, J.L., and K. Klokov. *Sustainable Reindeer Husbandry: Summary Report.* Arctic Council, 2000–2002. https://oaarchive.arctic-council. org/bitstream/handle/11374/1592/MM03_SDWG_Attachment_2. pdf?sequence=4&isAllowed=y.

Mikkleson, D. "Did Disney Fake Lemming Deaths for the Nature Documentary 'White Wilderness'?" *Snopes*, February 27, 1996. https:// www.snopes.com/fact-check/white-wilderness.

Nomadicare Mongolia. https://www.nomadicare.org/.

Rhys, P. "Sweden Reindeer Herders Face Revenge Attacks after Landmark Case." *Aljazeera*, April 25, 2020. https://www.aljazeera.com/ news/2020/04/sweden-reindeer-herders-face-revenge-attacks-land- mark-case-200425154622046.html.

Rowat, A. "Ninja Mining in Mongolia's Far North." *Bloomberg*, March 6, 2012. https://www.bloomberg.com/news/photo-essays/2012-03-06/ ninja-mining-in-mongolias-far-north.

Skarin, A., et al. "Wind Farm Construction Impacts Reindeer Migration and Movement Corridors." *Landscape Ecology* 30 (2015): 1527–1540. https:// doi.org/10.1007/s10980-015-0210-8.

Skarin, A., P. Sandström, and A. Moudud. "Out of Sight of Wind Turbines— Reindeer Response to Wind Farms in Operation." *Ecology and Evolution* 8, no. 19 (October 2018): 9906–9919. https://doi.org/10.1002/ece3.4476.

Smith, T. *The Real Rudolph: A Natural History of Reindeer*. Stroud, UK: Sutton Publishing Ltd., 2006.

Strzyżyńska, W. "Sámi Reindeer Herders File Lawsuit against Norway Windfarm." *The Guardian*, January 18, 2021. https://www.theguardian.com/world/2021/jan/18/sami-reindeer-herders-file-lawsuit-against-oyfjellet-norway-windfarm-project.

Sweeney, N. "The Dukha: Last of Mongolia's Reindeer People." *CNN*, September 29, 2016. https://www.cnn.com/travel/article/dukha-last-reindeer-people/index.html.

Taylor, W., et al. "Investigating Reindeer Pastoralism and Exploitation of High Mountain Zones in Northern Mongolia through Ice Patch Archaeology." *PLOS ONE*, November 20, 2019. https://journals.plos.org/plosone/article?id=10.1371/journal.pone.0224741.

Tyler, N.J.C., et al. "The Shrinking Resource Base of Pastoralism: Saami Reindeer Husbandry in a Climate of Change." *Frontiers in Sustainable Food Systems*, February 10, 2021. https://doi.org/10.3389/fsufs.2020.585685.

Chapter 27: COVID

The Cairngorm Reindeer Herd: Roaming Freely since 1952. https://www.cairngormreindeer.co.uk.

Index

Jerry Haigh is a Kenya-born, Glasgow-schooled veterinarian, who lives in Canada's province of Saskatchewan. Three days after graduation in Scotland, he returned to Africa and within three days was confronted with a lame giraffe. During the ten years he spent there, and several return trips, he worked on many species of wildlife in six countries. In 1975 he moved with his family from Kenya to Saskatoon to a position as a wildlife veterinarian at the Western College of Veterinary Medicine. For a further 34 years, he worked with a wide variety of exotic animals, both in zoos and free-ranging environments in Canada and other parts of the world. These included polar bears, seals, moose, caribou and reindeer, and several species of deer in a number of countries. For seven years he and his doctor wife Jo took vet students to Uganda to study the complex relationship between humans, livestock and wildlife.

He has written a textbook on deer faming and four nonfiction books, as well as many magazine articles. His website (www.jerryhaigh.com) offers snippets from each of these and has links to other things he enjoys, which include storytelling, photography and woodworking. Other activities include visits to the theatre, reading, fishing, canoeing and hunting. He has served as president of the American College of Zoological Medicine and the Saskatchewan Writers' Guild.